BASIC RESEARCH METHODS

An Entry to Qualitative and Quantitative Research

Dr. Peter Kibet

Description

This e-book offers a comprehensive rounded view of research as a tool for problem-solving. The purpose of this e-book is to promote an understanding of basic research for college and university students in all fields. It covers terms which are used in research, ethical Issues in Research with Children, research designs and methodologies, selection of appropriate research design methodologies, data analysis procedures, and how to write a research proposal.

About the author

Dr. Peter Kibet is a lecturer at Machakos University Department of Early Childhood Education where he teaches courses in reading, language arts and developmental psychology for undergraduate, masters and PhD students. Previously, Kibet taught at Kenyatta University, Mt. Kenya University and Ndalat High School. He has 23 years experience teaching in high school and University. He has published widely in referred journals.

Table of content

Contents

CHAPTER ONE

DEFINITION OF RESEARCH TERMS

1.0 Introduction

A definition is a passage that explains the meaning of a term (a word, phrase, or other set of symbols), or a type of thing. The term to be defined is the definiendum. A term may have many different senses or meanings. For each such specific sense, a definiens is a cluster of words that defines that term. The chief difficulty in managing definition is the need to use other terms that are already understood or whose definitions are easily obtainable. The use of the term in a simple example may suffice. By contrast, a dictionary definition has additional details, typically including an etymology showing areas of usage (snapshots) of the earlier meanings and the parent language. Like any other word, the term definition has subtly different meanings in different contexts.

1.1 Definition of terms

Definition is a statement explaining the meaning of a word or expression especially in a dictionary. Another meaning is that a Definition is the quality of being clear and distinct. In research we need to give the definition of the words that may be misinterpreted and again because we would like to be very clear and quite distinct in what we are telling others through our studies. Here below is a set of definitions of words, expressions and term mostly used in research studies.

1.2 Research

The Dictionary definition of the term *Research* is "a detailed study of a subject or an aspect of a subject." As described in our introduction above we need to see how scholars have treated this term and other terms in order to arrive at their solution to their problems of study. Research has variously been defined by different scholars.

a) A broad definition of research is given by Martin Shuttleworth - "In the broadest sense of the word, the definition of research includes any gathering of data, information and facts for the advancement of knowledge.

b) Another definition of research is given by Creswell who states - "Research is a process of steps used to collect and analyze information to increase our understanding of a topic or issue". It consists of three steps: Pose a question, collect data to answer the question, and present an answer to the question.

c) The Merriam-Webster Online Dictionary defines research in more detail as "a studious inquiry or examination; especially : investigation or experimentation aimed at the discovery and interpretation of facts, revision of accepted theories or laws in the light of new facts, or practical application of such new or revised theories or laws".

d) Kombo and Tromp (2006)say, that the term "research" means to look for, examine, investigate or explore, and Orodho and Kombo (2002*)* define research as the process

1

of arriving at dependable solutions to problems through a planned systematic collection, analysis and interpretation of data.

Generally, **Research** is said to be a systematic investigation into existing or new knowledge. It is used to establish or confirm facts, reaffirm the results of previous work, solve new or existing problems, support theorems, or develop new theories. A research project may also be an expansion on past work in the field. In order to test the validity of instruments, procedures, or experiments, research may replicate elements of prior projects, or the project as a whole. The primary purposes of basic research (as opposed to applied research) are documentation, discovery, interpretation, or the research and development of methods and systems for the advancement of human knowledge. Approaches to research depend on epistemologies, which vary considerably both within and between humanities and sciences. There are several forms of research: scientific, humanities, artistic, economic, social, business, etc.

Although there are many ways we study problems, there are two ways to conduct Research study:

1) Primary research: Using primary sources, i.e., original documents and data.
2) Secondary Research: Using secondary sources, i.e., a synthesis of, interpretation of, or discussions about primary sources.

In dealing with the two ways of conducting research, the two very common approaches reaching the solution or answers to our research questions is through data/information collection, analysis and interpretation of the findings.

There are two major research approaches or plans so called designs to help us get that far: **qualitative** research and **quantitative** research. Researchers choose one of these two tracks according to the nature of the research problem they want to observe and the research questions they aim to answer or they combine the two if the information collected warrants the combination of the methods.

1.3 Qualitative Research

Understanding of human behavior and the reasons that govern such behavior. Asking a broad question and collecting word-type data that is analyzed searching for themes. This type of research looks to describe a population without attempting to quantifiably measure variables or look to potential relationships between variables. It is viewed as more restrictive in testing hypotheses because it can be expensive and time consuming, and typically limited to a single set of research subjects. Qualitative research is often used as a method of exploratory research as a basis for later quantitative research hypotheses.

1.4 Quantitative Research

Systematic empirical investigation of quantitative properties and phenomena and their relationships. Asking a narrow question and collecting numerical data to analyze utilizing statistical methods. The quantitative research designs are experimental, correlational, and survey (or descriptive). Statistics derived from quantitative research can be used to establish the existence of associative or causal relationships between variables. The Quantitative data collection methods rely on random sampling and structured data collection instruments that fit diverse experiences into predetermined response categories. These methods produce results that are easy to summarize, compare, and generalize. Quantitative research is concerned with testing hypotheses derived from theory and/or being able to estimate the size of a phenomenon of interest. Depending on the research question, participants may be randomly assigned to different treatments (this is the only way that a quantitative study can be considered a true experiment). If this is not feasible, the researcher may collect data on participant and situational characteristics in order to statistically control for their influence on the dependent, or outcome, variable. If the intent is to generalize from the research participants to a larger population, the researcher will employ probability sampling to select participants. Each of these research forms demands different *research design model(s)*.

1.5 Research Design

This is a method, a plan, a structure or a strategy a researcher considers most appropriate to use to investigate research questions in his/her research study in order to come up with a solution(s) or an answer(s) to the research problem(s) or question(s) envisaged. That is, a Research Design is a plan so designed as to offer the kind of route an Investigator has to follow and type of activities that will take place en-route in order to find a solution or solutions to identified problem(s). It is a Method a Researcher plans to use to collect data (information), to organize and analyze that information into comprehensible results.

Research designs fall into two broad classes:-**Experimental** and **Quasi-experimental** where experimental studies are characterized by the ability to randomize subjects into treatment and control groups.

1.6 Hypothesis

"A hypothesis is a logical supposition, a reasonable guess, an educated conjecture. It provides a tentative *explanation* for a phenomenon under investigation." (Leedy and Ormrod, 2001). Or a hypothesis is a tentative answer to a research problem. The hypotheses are tentative because they can only be verified only after they have been tested scientifically. OR Research hypotheses are the specific testable predictions made about the independent and dependent variables in the study. Usually the literature review has given background material that justifies the particular hypotheses that are to be tested. Hypotheses are couched in terms of the particular independent and dependent variables that are going to be used in the study. *An example would be:*

> *"Children who are exposed to regular singing of the alphabet will show greater recognition of letters than children who are exposed to regular pronouncing of the alphabet".*

Notice also that this research hypothesis specifies a direction in that it predicts that the singing group will recognize more letters than the pronouncing group. This is not always the case. Research hypotheses can also specify a difference without saying which group will be better than the other. In general, it is considered a better hypothesis if you can specify a direction.

Finally, note the deductive reasoning principle of the scientific method when we test hypotheses. If our theories and ideas are the truth we can devise controlled experiments and find evidence to support them. This gives considerable credence to our theories. If we work the other way, and gather data first and then try to work out what happened (inductive reasoning) we could be faced with a large number of competing theories all of which could be true or not true. This is sometimes called posthoc theorizing and is a common way in which people explain events in their world. But we have no way of knowing which one is correct, we have no way of ruling out the competing reasons and we usually end up with choosing the one that fits best with our existing biases. Inductive reasoning does have a role in exploratory research in order to develop initial ideas and hypotheses, but in the end the hypotheses have to be tested before they can have scientific credence. In research, an investigator is able to either support or reject a hypothesis. If a hypothesis is rejected, it will lead an investigator to new hypothesis to explain the phenomenon in question. If a hypothesis is continually supported, it may evolve into a theory (Leedy and Ormrod, 2001).

A hypothesis could be stated as a *null hypothesis* or *alternate hypothesis*. Examples of these statements are given here below.*A null hypothesis* is a statement that shows no relationship between variable. For example there is no relationship between parents IQ and Child's IQ.*An alternate hypothesis* is a statement that predicts a relationship between two variables. For example there is relationship between children's IQ and the children's IQ.

1.7Variables

Any factor that can take on different values is a scientific variable and influences the outcome of experimental research. Gender, color and country are all perfectly acceptable variables, because they are inherently changeable. Most scientific experiments measure quantifiable factors, such as time or weight, but this is not essential for a component to be classed as a variable.

As an example, most of us have filled in surveys where a researcher asks questions and asks you to rate answers. These responses generally have a numerical range, from   '1 – Strongly Agree' through to '5 – Strongly Disagree'. This type of measurement allows opinions to be statistically analyzed and evaluated. There are many types of variable but the most important for the vast majority   of   research   methods,   are   the ***Dependent   and   Independent   Variables***. The key to designing any experiment is to look at what research variables could affect the outcome. A researcher must determine which variable needs to be manipulated to generate quantifiable results.

The independent variable is the core of the experiment and is isolated and manipulated by the researcher. The dependent variable is the measurable outcome of this manipulation, the results of the experimental design. For many physical experiments, isolating the independent variable and

4

measuring the dependent is generally easy.   If you designed an experiment to determine how quickly a cup of coffee cools, the manipulated independent variable is time and the dependent measured variable is temperature. In other fields of science, the variables are often more difficult to determine and an experiment needs a robust design. Operationalization is a useful tool to measure fuzzy concepts which do not have one obvious variable.   .

a) *An independent variable* is the variable that is manipulated by the researcher to see how it affects the dependent variable.

b) *A dependent variable* is that variable that changes as a result of a change in the independent variable. It is the behavior or response outcome that the researcher measures which is hoped to have been affected by the independent variable.

c) *An extraneous variable* is any variable other than the independent valuable that may influence the independent variable in a specific way

d) *A control variable* is that variable that is held constant in order to examine whether the effects of the relationship between independent variable and dependent variable are by chance.

1.8 Operational Definition

An **operational definition** defines something (e.g. a variable, term, or object) in terms of the specific process or set of validation tests used to determine its presence and quantity. That is, one defines something in terms of *the operations that count as measuring it.* The term was coined by Percy Williams Bridgman and is a part of the process of operationalization. One might use definitions that rely on operations in order to avoid the troubles associated with attempting to define things in terms of some intrinsic essence.

An example of an operational definition might be defining the weight of an object in terms of the numbers that appear when that object is placed on a weighing scale. The weight then, is whatever results from following *the (weight) measurement procedure,* which should be repeatable by anyone. This is in contrast to Operationalization that uses theoretical definitions. Despite the controversial philosophical origins of the concept, particularly its close association with logical positivism, operational definitions have undisputed practical applications. This is especially so in the social and medical sciences, where operational definitions of key terms are used to preserve the unambiguous empirical testability of hypothesis and theory. Operational definitions   are also important in the physical sciences.

In child and family studies, most times we tend to use operational definitions due to   the operationalization of the situations, surrounding the child and the family, situations which are never static to the person, child's or family's interactive activities. Such operational definitions help the researchers to come up with predictable results.

CHAPTER TWO

ETHICAL ISSUES IN RESEARCH WITH CHILDREN

2.0 Introduction

In this article, we are going to look at some of the ethical issues that one should consider when doing a research with children. This will also prepare you for your research that you will undertake after course work. The article will also give insights on the frequently asked questions.

2.1 The Ethics of Research with Children

Efforts to improve the health of children depend on clinical investigations that use children as research subjects. Children are a vulnerable population, however, and so are accorded special protection from research risks. Researchers in pediatrics may encounter conflicts between protecting the children who are vulnerable research subjects and developing generalizable knowledge to benefit children as a class. Furthermore, there are many pitfalls for the researcher in carrying out the communication with both parents and children that is required for responsible decision making about participation by children or adolescents in experiments.

There is a long standing moral and legal tradition that supports parents as the primary decision makers for their minor children, including the right to make proxy decisions for children about participation in research. Parental decision making is a critical factor in the study of pediatric research ethics, even though it is recognized that parents, as well as health researchers, may have interests that conflict with the best interests of the child.

Today, the legitimate role of the child in decisions about research participation is recognized. The ethical concept of assent provides a framework to assist investigators and parents with efforts to incorporate the views of children who are recruited as research subjects. Assent is analogous to consent where the subject has a reduced capacity to understand the matter to which they are assenting. This lecture covers the key issues that arise when research is conducted with children as subjects.

2.1.1 Parents as Primary Decision Makers for Children

Historically, the rights of parents over children were grounded in the property rights of fathers. Children were little more than paternal property, so fathers exercised nearly complete control, with few, if any, external limits. Today, several other reasons have emerged to explain why parents are considered the most appropriate decision makers for their children. First, parents are responsible for the welfare of their children, and this implies not only the right, but the duty, for parents to make decisions on their child's behalf. Second, parents are the parties who live most closely with the consequences of their child rearing decisions. Third, parents teach their children values and, as a consequence, it is highly likely that the child will have the value commitments that resemble those of their parents. Lastly, society gives moral weight to the maintenance of family life and recognizes the need to protect those relationships from outside interference unless grave harm is being done.

2.1.2 Ethical Issues in Human Subject Research

There are several ethical issues that must be considered when designing research that will utilize participants who are human beings.

- The primary concern of the investigator should be the safety of the research participant. This is accomplished by carefully considering the risk/benefit ratio, using all available information to make an appropriate assessment and continually monitoring the research as it proceeds.
- The scientific investigator must obtain informed consent from each research participant. This should be obtained in writing (although oral consents are sometimes acceptable) after the participant has had the opportunity to carefully consider the risks and benefits and to ask any pertinent questions. Informed consent should be seen as an ongoing process, not a singular event or a mere formality.
- The investigator must enumerate how privacy and confidentiality concerns will be approached. Researchers must be sensitive to not only how information is protected from unauthorized observation, but also if and how participants are to be notified of any unforeseen findings from the research that they may or may not want to know.
- The investigator must consider how adverse events will be handled; who will provide care for a participant injured in a study and who will pay for that care are important considerations.
- In addition, before enrolling participants in an experimental trial, the investigator should be in a state of "equipoise," that is, if a new intervention is being tested against the currently accepted treatment, the investigator should be genuinely uncertain which approach is superior. In other words, a true null hypothesis should exist at the onset regarding the outcome of the trial.

Ethical principles governing research with human subjects
There are three primary ethical principles that are traditionally cited when discussing ethical concerns in human subject research. (A more complete enumeration of these principles is available in the Belmont Report, written by The National Commission for the Protection of Human Subjects of Biomedical and Behavioral Research in 1979.)

- The first ethical principle cited by the influential Belmont Report is autonomy, which refers to the obligation on the part of the investigator to respect each participant as a person capable of making an informed decision regarding participation in the research study. The investigator must ensure that the participant has received a full disclosure of the nature of the study, the risks, benefits and alternatives, with an extended opportunity to ask questions. The principle of autonomy finds expression in the informed consent document.

- The second ethical principle is beneficence, which refers to the obligation on the part of the investigator to attempt to maximize benefits for the individual participant and/or society, while minimizing risk of harm to the individual. An honest and thorough risk/benefit calculation must be performed.

7

- The third ethical principle involved in research with human subjects is justice, which demands equitable selection of participants, i.e., avoiding participant populations that may be unfairly coerced into participating, such as prisoners and institutionalized children. The principle of justice also requires equality in distribution of benefits and burdens among the population group(s) likely to benefit from the research.

2.2 Components of An Ethically Valid Informed Consent For Research

For an informed consent to be ethically valid, the following components must be present:

- *Disclosure:* The potential participant must be informed as fully as possible of the nature and purpose of the research, the procedures to be used, the expected benefits to the participant and/or society, the potential of reasonably foreseeable risks, stresses, and discomforts, and alternatives to participating in the research. There should also be a statement that describes procedures in place to ensure the confidentiality or anonymity of the participant. The informed consent document must also disclose what compensation and medical treatment are available in the case of a research related injury. The document should make it clear whom to contact with questions about the research study, research subjects' rights, and in case of injury.
- *Understanding:* The participant must understand what has been explained and must be given the opportunity to ask questions and have them answered by one of the investigators. The informed consent document must be written in lay language, avoiding any technical jargon.
- *Voluntariness:* The participant's consent to participate in the research must be voluntary, free of any coercion or promises of benefits unlikely to result from participation.
- *Competence:* The participant must be competent to give consent. If the participant is not competent due to mental status, disease, or emergency, a designated surrogate may provide consent if it is in the participant's best interest to participate. In certain emergency cases, consent may be waived due to the lack of a competent participant and a surrogate.
- *Consent:* The potential human subject must authorize his/her participation in the research study, preferably in writing, although at times an oral consent or assent may be more appropriate.

2.3 Deception in Doing Research

As a general rule, deception is not acceptable when doing research with humans. Using deception jeopardizes the integrity of the informed consent process and can potentially harm your participants. Occasionally exploring your area of interest fully may require misleading your participants about the subject of your study. For example, if you want to learn about decision making practices of physicians without influencing their practice style, you may consider telling them you are studying "communication behaviors" more broadly. The IRB will review any proposal that suggests using deception or misrepresentation very carefully. They will require an in depth justification of why the deception is necessary for the study and the steps you will take to safeguard your participants.

CHAPTER TWO

PROPOSAL WRITING

2.0 Introduction

The first step in social research is often that of finding out what is already known. Because of the increase of social research publications, you need to learn how to use   most efficient research procedures, several of which are described in many social science research texts. Increasingly, you will rely on computer procedures for locating books and journal articles on particular topics. These electronics techniques provide the speed necessary to search huge databases. Once you have identified a relevant area of study, you need to read it critically and widely. Fortunately, social research journals follow a fairly standard format, which makes it easy for one to find the part one needs within the whole report.

2.1 Research Proposal

Guidelines for Writing a Proposal (or Project Proposal) are set out according to the kind of research or project that is to be undertaken. However, in any of the proposals, there are some common areas or chapters that must feature.
Let us look for guidelines for writing a **funding project proposal** first. These guidelines reflect the objectives and **funding criteria** of all programs. Due to their general nature, some of the subcategories may not apply in every case. The guidelines cover the major categories required in a proposal and address some general questions concerning the proposed structure and content of the documentation.

A proposal's maximum length can be discussed with Funding program officer. Generally, it is preferred that the research proposal, excluding appendices, should not exceed 20 single-spaced pages. Proposals may be submitted in English or any other agreed language between the researcher and the Donor. In non-funded proposals, usually the language used is English.

2.3 Project overview

- **Title**: This should be a short phrase describing the subject of the proposal. Be sure to provide the name of the research organization, the name of the project leader, and collaborating research organizations.
- **Estimated budget:** Estimate the total cost of the project in national currency.
- **Estimated duration:** Indicate how many months it will take to complete the entire project, including writing and submitting the final reports.
- **Objectives:** Indicate both the general and specific objectives of the project.
- **Abstract:** Provide a summary of 150 to 300 words of the problem, how it will be studied, the expected results, and how they will be used.

2.4 Administrative information

- **Project leader:** Name the person(s) who would have the main responsibility for the technical and administrative coordination of the project. Include the project leader's title, address, work and home telephone numbers, cable/telex and fax numbers, and email address (if available). Proposals to establish a research network should include the name of the network's coordinator and the institution where the network will be located.
- **Recipient institution:** Name the recipient organization that will administer the research funds. The recipient institution must be a recognized legal entity that is capable of entering into contractual arrangements and assuming legal obligations. Include the institution's address, telephone, cable/telex, and fax numbers, and email address (if available). Note that researchers must be affiliated with an institution to receive a grant.
- **Collaborating institution:** Identify any co-submitter of the proposal that will also enter into a contractual relationship with Donor as recipient institution (co-recipient).
- **Participating institution:** In some cases, all or part of the research may be carried out in an institution other than the recipient institution administering the funds. Give the names and addresses of any participating institutions.
- **Other donor agencies** (if any) funding this proposal: Provide the names and a description of the roles of other agencies and, if known, the amount they will contribute.
- **Other donor agencies** (if any) to whom this proposal was submitted for independent funding: Provide the name(s) of any other agency currently considering this proposal for funding.
- **Supporting administrative documents:** The institution's responsible officer should attach a letter of formal request for support from the Donor when the final research proposal is submitted. (The responsible officer is the person authorized to submit official requests for funding on behalf of the institution, such as the Vice Chancellor of a university, the head of a government department, or the executive officer of a non-governmental organization.) In cases where the research leader and the responsible officer are the same, please have the responsible financial officer of the institution submit or co-sign the formal request.

In cases where there has been no previous collaboration between the institutions presenting the proposal and the Donor, a copy of the document certifying the legal status of the institution should be attached to the proposal. In cases where there are collaborating institutions, please submit a document certifying collaboration.

As noted earlier, many countries require that government approval be obtained for outside funding of research projects. This may apply even if that funding is not going to a government institution. Where such clearance is required, Donor cannot fund any project until a copy of the official approval document has been submitted to the Donor.

2.5 Problem and justification

This section should normally make up between one-quarter and one-half of the proposal. It should describe the problem that is to be investigated and the questions that will guide the research process. Note that proper justification of the importance of the research questions to be addressed requires some sense of the likely contribution to knowledge that the research will make and its place in current debate or technological advance. Often, this can be presented in the form of research hypotheses to be tested. This section should provide a brief overview of the literature and research done in the field related to the problem, and of the gaps that the proposed research is intended to fill. To show the importance of the problem, this section may discuss such points as:

- How the research relates to the development priorities of the country or countries concerned;
- The scientific importance of the problem;
- The magnitude of the problem and how the research results will contribute to its solution;
- The special importance of the project for vulnerable social groups; and
- The need to build up research capacity in the proposed area of research.

Note that Proposals should be explicit about the objectives that the project will address.

If the proposal is for the second phase of a project or if the applicant has received Donor's funding in the past for similar work, describe the results of the previous work and indicate why additional work is required.

2.5.1 A note on technological research

If one of the project's objectives is to produce a prototype of a "hard" or "soft" technology and there are reasonable expectations that it will be widely distributed and marketed, the proposal should discuss the socioeconomic implications:

- **Demand and supply:** the expected level of demand for the technology; marketing requirements; users' willingness or ability to pay; alternative sources of supply; price and quality competitiveness; input and credit availability; pricing policies.
- **Profitability:** the financial viability for entrepreneurs, farmers, or consumers; cost-effectiveness compared to alternatives.
- **Social impact:** the impact on working conditions or quality of life; distribution of benefits between income classes and genders; degree and nature of local participation; effect on culture and values; long-term sustainability; the costs and benefits to society (for example, implications for government subsidies, tariff protection, pollution, taxes, skill, employment generation, savings, etc.).

2.5.2 Objectives

- The objectives section of a proposal is typically very brief, usually a half-page at most. This is because the rationale for each objective will already have been established in the previous section, while the ways of achieving the objectives should be explained in the methodology section.
- The **General objectives** provide a short statement of the development goal being pursued by the research.

- The **Specific objectives** are operational in nature. They may indicate specific types of knowledge to be produced, certain audiences to be reached, and certain forms of capacity to be reinforced. These are the objectives against which the success of the project will be judged. It is important to distinguish the specific objectives from the means of achieving them, such as pursuing field work, organizing a network or a workshop, or publishing a book.

2.6 Methodology

It is best to organize the methodology to explain how each specific objective will be achieved. The proposal should provide enough detail to enable an independent scientific assessment of the proposal. Assuming that the research questions and research hypotheses to be addressed by the project have been clearly identified in the "Problem and justification" section, the purpose of the methodology section is to show how these questions will be answered in the most rigorous way possible.

The methodology section deserves greater emphasis than applicants typically give it. The proposals needs to be clear about what activities are envisaged in the pursuit of each objective, and this must be done before funding is approved. Indeed, it is impossible to define the budgetary needs of the project in the absence of a solid methodology section.

Conceptual and theoretical framework: The proposed research may be exploratory or highly structured, quantitative or qualitative. In all cases, however, the methodology section should begin by defining the conceptual framework and theoretical frame of reference that will guide the research. The main explanatory and dependent variables should be identified and related one to another.

User participation: Participatory aspects of the project are often important. Indicate whether the ultimate users of the research results were involved in the design of the project and what role they will play in executing the project or in implementing the results.

Data collection: Proposals should indicate what approaches and methods will be used to collect primary and secondary data and information. Provide details on available sources of secondary data or the methods to be used to collect primary data, such as questionnaires and group discussions. Outline the procedures for the development, pretesting, and administration of any research instruments.

If survey work is involved, give detailed information on the study area. If the research is related to human populations, information on the study population should also be provided. Include a description of the procedures for selecting the population sample and the sample size. The survey sample should reflect ethical considerations to protect confidentiality and an appropriate gender balance among surveyors or those surveyed.

If biological samples are to be collected, provide information on the number and type of samples, the method of collection, who will perform the collection, and how the samples will be transported, stored, and analyzed.

If laboratory procedures are involved, standardized procedures and protocols must be stipulated (quote relevant references). Describe new or unique procedures in detail and specify the quality assurance procedures that will be followed.

Data analysis: Finally, describe what types of data analysis or modeling exercises will be carried out. Describe the procedures for processing and analyzing the data, including the project's needs for computer facilities.

Gender considerations: State whether gender considerations constitute an important dimension of the project in defining the important relationships of the problem or in data collection, and show explicitly how the methodology will address them.

Ethical considerations: Projects that involve research on human subjects, the collection of private or personal information, or the participation of individuals in experiments must be designed in ways that protect the privacy, dignity, and integrity of those who are the subjects of research.

For projects involving research on human subjects, which raise ethical issues, the Donor requires that an independent ethical review committee, whether in the recipient institution or in the host country, approve ethical protocols. This applies most often in health research. In these cases, please attach a document certifying that ethical approval has been given. The proposal should also provide detailed information on the ethical dimensions of the research and how these are being handled.

For projects involving the collection of corporate or personal information, the proposal should provide details on how informed consent will be obtained and how the information will be kept confidential.

For projects that involve individuals participating in an experiment (such as farmers testing a new farming practice or community members responding to group questioning), provide information on the free consent of participants and how it will be obtained. Outline how research findings will be reported back to the people concerned.

Training: Identify how the project might contribute to the training of staff and whether it would be necessary for certain staff to undergo training prior to or during the project. What kinds of training would be most appropriate (e.g., formal graduate training, non-formal skills upgrading course, visits or missions, etc.) and how it would be organized?

Organizational matters: For larger projects or networked initiatives, organizational elements are an essential part of the methodology, and may constitute an important part of the methodology section.

Collaborative arrangements with other institutions: In the case of collaborative projects with other institutions, give the reasons for collaboration with other researchers from other institutions. How will the cooperation between other researchers and researchers in your institution be organized? What will be the division of labor?

2.7 Results and dissemination

Begin by defining the major outputs expected from the project, while outlining plans for disseminating or implementing the findings of the proposed research. Examples of outputs include workshops and conferences, reports and publications, new methodologies or technologies, improved research skills, and the institutional reinforcement. Show how research results will be communicated to users and decision-makers. Discuss how research results are likely to be used. Identify the immediate or intermediate users of the results and show how they will be given access to the research results. Who will ultimately benefit if the project results are appropriately used?

The expected impact of research results can be discussed in reference to some or all of the following:

- their potential use in other settings;
- their contribution to existing technical and scientific knowledge;
- policy formulation and implementation;
- development processes at the local, national, and regional levels; and
- the needs of specific target populations.

Discuss any possible obstacles to the execution of the research and to the eventual use of the results. These may include possibilities of political or economic instability, expected difficulties in securing access to data, the difficulty of coming to categorical conclusions, and the partial nature of the results for addressing specific development problems.

A note on intellectual property

Research inevitably leads to the creation of intellectual property. Any Donor's policy is that written materials and documentation are owned by their creator, who also holds copyright. However, the Donor seeks the right to disseminate the information so that the benefits of the research will be circulated as widely as possible. If a technology is developed during a project, Donor's main objective is to ensure its dissemination and utilization. Where relevant, the recipient will be asked to sign a Memorandum of Understanding which sets out the ownership and royalty regimes that will govern the project.

Typically, the Donor's role is to help secure appropriate protection for intellectual property rights internationally, with the recipient having full licensing rights in all countries. Apart from recouping any costs of patenting, the Donor may wish to receive a share of any profit only in those cases where significant revenues may be generated. It is

14

the Donor's policy to recoup any grant given to a private sector company if the technology it develops is successful.

Institutions and personnel

Institutions: Briefly describe the research institution, including its history and objectives. Similarly, provide information on collaborating agencies and those institutions or agencies that have been involved in planning the research, that will be involved in carrying it out, and that will be asked for funds. Highlight the particular strengths or past achievements of the institution.

Describe previous or ongoing support to the person, unit, or institution in the field of research related to the proposal. How might the proposed research complement the institution's existing program?

Personnel: List the personnel who will be involved in carrying out the project, their roles, and their time commitments. Describe their qualifications, experience, or any other relevant information. Include the résumés of the principal professional staff.

2.8 Timetable and budget

2.8.1 Schedule and duration:

Setting the duration of a project has grave consequences in terms of fixing the times for different deliverables and the final report. Planning must be carried out following the most rigorous project management standards.   Indicate the time needed to carry out each phase of the project, as well as the project's total duration. Remember to take into account the time required for staff recruitment and equipment purchases. Indicate possible constraints in adhering to the timetable.

2.8.2 Budget:

The budget should be divided into two categories: the Donor's contribution and the local (recipient) contribution. The local contribution can be an estimate of "in kind" resources such as salaries, equipment, etc. The budget estimates mostly should be computed on an annual basis (a 12 month period). Estimate the project's total costs, indicating the annual contributions to be made by each institution or agency involved. Allow for inflation and indicate the level of inflation used in the estimate. All budget items must be quoted in national currencies. In certain cases, projects can be managed by activity or milestones. Identify outputs and estimate costs by output which should also have firm delivery dates. The following are brief descriptions of standard budget categories.(More details on budget preparation and reporting can be requested from the Donor-Institution.)

2.8.3 Personnel:

You can include under salaries all remuneration, allowances, honoraria, and benefits that are paid to project staff and advisors hired for your specific project. Project advisors are people hired for long periods (more than one year) and paid on a regular basis. Some Donors may pay the replacement cost (e.g. release time for academics) of principal researchers based on their time commitment to the project, their research role, and policy of your institution.

2.8.4 Consultants:

All expenses related to acquiring the services of a consultant for a specific activity within your project can be included in this category. Costs may include fees, travel, accommodation, living expenses, and support services hired directly by the consultant and billed to your project. You should indicate the total cost for each consultant as a single lump sum, and use a note to give a breakdown of the costs.

2.8.5 Equipment:

Within this category you can include all equipment that has a useful life of more than one year. Costs may include the basic purchase price, related sales taxes, freight costs, and other costs associated with purchasing the equipment. Most Donors do not pay import duties or insurance on equipment after it is delivered to you.

2.8.6 International travel:

This category includes costs for ground transportation, accommodation, meals, airfare, departure taxes, and other expenses related to international travel by project staff. You must use your institution's own travel-management processes to handle travel, but the class of travel must follow Donor's policy on travel issues.

2.8.7 Research expenses:

All costs related to carrying out the research and disseminating the findings should be recorded as research expenses. These costs may include such items as payments to people who gather data or provide casual labor, the maintenance and operation of project vehicles, consumable goods and non-capital equipment, computer services, in-country travel, reference materials, rent paid for land or premises used in a research project, conference registration, dissemination costs, seminar and conference equipment rental, and printing.

2.8.8 Evaluation:

You should include here all costs related to systematic assessments that either estimate or measure progress toward achieving project objectives or the quality and effects of funded activities. You can include costs for consultant fees, travel expenses and the dissemination of evaluation findings. In projects where evaluation is the primary objective, costs can also include research expenses, training, and salaries and benefits for personnel directly involved in the evaluation.

o **Training:** Under this category you should include all expenses related to registration, tuition fees, living allowances, research and training expenses, and travel costs to undertake the training. These costs should be reported under four categories: PhD degree; Master's degree; Short Course (e.g., a diploma or certificate); and other (e.g., field work or postdoctoral study). Please note that you should include training for project staff that is directly related to the implementation of research activities under "Research expenses". **Indirect costs:** Here you should include administrative costs not directly related to the research. These costs should be specified in the grant agreement and can include such items as:
  - clerical, accounting, or secretarial help;
  - general office expenses;
  - office rental and utility charges;
  - non-capital office furnishings;
  - communications costs; and
  - photocopying.

Note: A budget note is required for each line item in the budget. The budget notes should state exactly what is covered under the heading and the basis on which the budgeted amount was calculated.

2.9 Evaluation

Certain projects benefit from more extensive evaluation than that corresponding to normal management and monitoring. Such cases include projects that are particularly innovative or risky, those from which significant lessons can be learned, and those that require a very high level of accountability. Indicate if the project will include an explicit evaluation component.

A description of the evaluation component should:

- identify who will use the evaluation findings and for what purpose(s);
- focus on a few specific issues that are well defined and relate directly to the project's objectives and activities;
- specify the methods by which data will be collected; and
- identify the resources necessary for the evaluation.

2.10 Appendices

Attach any supporting documents such as maps, the resumes of personnel, or bibliographies.
To summarize all that regarding Funded Project proposal writing, let us look at a Format.

Karamu Youth Education Foundation Project Proposal Format

GENERAL INFORMATION

1. Name of Organization
2. Project Title
3. Project Location
4. Contact Person
5. Contact Information: Physical Address, Postal Address, Phone Number and Email Address
6. Project Timeline
7. Amount Requested

EXECUTIVE SUMMARY:

Provide a brief overview and summary of the project. It should provide a credible statement that describes your organization and establish the significance of the project

PROBLEM STATEMENT:

State the challenges identified, the rationale/need to address these challenges and the conditions to be changed by the project

PROJECT OBJECTIVES:

The objectives should describe the intended outcome of the project and should be SMART (Simple, Measurable, Accurate, Realistic and Time Bound) . Indicate how the objectives will contribute to the achievement of the project, what difference the project will make and the time frame during which this will happen.

PROJECT IMPLEMENTATION AND MANAGEMENT PLAN:

Describe the project activities indicating how the objectives will be accomplished, what will be done, who will do it, who are the implementers, partners and beneficiaries and when it will be done. Describe how the project will be sustainable after the funding period.

PROJECT MONITORING AND EVALUATION:

Describe how you are going to monitor and evaluate the project so as to assess progress during implementation and improve the project efficiency as the project moves along.

DOCUMENTATION AND SHARING RESULTS:

Describe how you are going to document the progress of your project during and after implementation. State how you will document and share your results and let others know of your purpose, methods and achievements.

PROJECT BUDGET:

Indicate the total cost of the project and also provide a detailed budget for these costs.

ANY ADDITIONAL INFORMATION:

Provide any additional information in support of this proposal application

After completing your proposal in the above format submit it to the Donor: *This time to*
Karamu Youth Education Foundation, Rhino Hse ; Suite #12
P.O. Box 817-10101,
Karatina Kenya
Or *email: theacademy03@ yahoo.com*

However on the usual academic researcher proposal writing a few of some features that have appeared in the above format will not be there and instead other features will prominently appear.

As described by Kombo and Tromp (2006) a research proposal means to put forward, suggest, intend or advise. A proposal therefore refers to suggestions, intentions, plans or schemes. Research proposals can consequently be referred to as a research plan, suggestion or request. It is a plan since it puts forward for consideration one's plan for intent. It is suggestion as it attempts to persuade people reading it to do something. This is either to fund a study, recommend that research should be carried out or to recommend the implementation of a project. Therefore a research proposal is a request to implement the study.

In order to come up with a well planned proposal, the concept of objectivity is very crucial. Objectivity is a characteristic of scientific research, which dictates that the procedures and subject matter of investigations should be planned in such way that language flow and all findings are put in their rightful place in the report to be written.

This calls for the knowledge and understanding of the parts and content of a research proposal. Although a proposal is a suggestion of intended research activity, the knowledge of how to write it is the beginning of how to write a report after the research is done. After the research study is done only two chapters are added to the proposal in order to come up with a research report.

It is after the manipulation of the data through the stated relationship of variables in the hypothesis that interpretation of the analysis is done and a report is written. In sections that follow, we are going to see how a proposal for intended research is done and how a report of the whole proposed research is written after the research process is concluded. This final report is called a Thesis and it differs from the proposal significantly.

Important parts of a Research Proposal.

    a)   ***Proposal Main Features***
    1   ***Cover Title page***
    This page consist of the following:
    Title (Topic of Research)
    Author (s) identification
    Caption (indication of why the study)

Date

2.   Declaration

The declaration is made by the student and the supervisor.

3.   Abstract

It summarizes the entire proposal, pointing out the research problem, the objective of the study and methods of data analysis. It should not exceed 500 words.

4.   Abbreviations and acronyms

This section should be included in the proposal only if it is applicable.

5.   Table of contents

It lists the chapter and section headings with their corresponding page numbers.

6.   Chapter 1

Introduction or Background of the research study. Other components of this chapter include: Statement of the problem, Purpose and objective of the study, Research questions and hypothesis, Significance of the study, Location of the study, Limitations of the study, Assumptions of the study, Conceptual and Theoretical Framework and Operational definitions (if any).

7.   Chapter 2

Literature review. This chapter is very important as you will be able to see what other researchers have done in the past regarding your area of research and what gaps that have been left, like the one you are about to study. Also this chapter is where you study the nature of research studies that are related to the one you are about to undertake. This helps you not to be a victim of plagrism. That is, duplicating other people's work.

8.   Chapter 3

Methodology Chapter is where you discuss all about the research design(s) you use to collect, organize and analyze research data. Also the research tools you use to help you collect relevant data

9.   References

10.   Appendices

b)   Research Report

1.   Cover page

   This page is similar with proposal in the title and author's identification. However the caption changes to: Research (Report) Thesis submitted for the degree of master of education in the school or faculty of ... then specify the Institution.

2.   Declaration

   This is similar to the proposal except that the word proposal is replaced with thesis or Research Project

3.   Dedication

4.   Acknowledgement

5.   Abstract

This should consist of the precise summary of the Proposal, Project or Thesis and it includes the objective of the study, Research design(s) and Methodologies used to collect, organize and analyze the data, the expected findings, discussion summary and recommendations in the conclusion.

6   Abbreviations and Acronyms

   Explain all abbreviations and acronyms as used in the entire thesis.

7.   Table of contents

It indicates all the chapter and section headings with their corresponding page numbers

8   **Chapter 1-3**
.Here the future tenses used in the proposal changes to past tense
9. **Chapter 4**
Data organization, analysis and discussion are put here.

10. **Chapter 5**
In this chapter, we have Summary, conclusion and recommendations

11. **References**
This part helps the reader to know the descriptions of previous knowledge and the part of researcher's additions knowledge.

12. **Appendices** This present research instruments, charts, graphs, budget, illustrations, etc.

Chapters of a Research Proposal

The chapters in a Research proposal are mainly three and here below their main features are included.

Chapter 1. Introduction
1.1 Background of the study
1.2 Statement of the problem
1.3 Purpose and objective of the study
1.4 Research questions and hypothesis
1.5 Significance of the study
1.6 Limitations of the study
1.7 Assumptions of the study
1.8 Conceptual/Theoretical Framework
1.9 Definition of terms

Chapter 2   Literature review
This consists of highlights of current studies that address the issues in the proposal. Clear gaps in quoted studies should be indicated

Chapter 3   Methodology
This chapter highlights the methodology appropriate to the study. i.e.
3.1   Research Design
3.2   Location of the Study
3.3   Target Population
3.4   Sample Selection
3.5   Research Instruments
3.6   Data Collection Techniques
3.7   Data Analysis

Differences between a Proposal and a Thesis
The major differences between a thesis and proposal are:

1. The use of future tenses in the writing of the proposal changes to past tense in the writing of the Thesis or Research Report.
2. In thesis there are more than three (3) chapters. The additional chapter four (4) is for details in data analysis, results and discussion. It includes:
    i) methods of data analysis
    ii) Results of descriptive and or inferential statistics
    iii) Discussion that amounts to interpretation of the analyzed data
3. Also in the Thesis or Research Report there is Chapter 5 which has summary, conclusion and recommendations as the main contents.

a) summary

Summary is based on results from the study .It is brief. All statements are concise, and pinpoint to the contributions that the researcher has made in the whole process. All statements are factual One way to represent the summary is to use one paragraph for each idea or alternatively, the researcher can use a point by point format in discussing the contributions done in the research study.

b) Conclusion

The conclusion section should be brief indicating what the study results reaffirm or negate, whichever was being investigated and the outcome of the investigation. It should briefly discuss some of the strategies highlighted by the respondents. In this section the researcher should clearly state how the study has contributed to knowledge relevant to the research study that was carried out.

c) Recommendations

The recommendations section is important in research. This section often exposes further problems and introduces more questions. As a researcher here is time limit to the research project, so it is unlikely that the study would have solved all the problems associated with the area of study. The researcher is therefore expected to make suggestions about how his /her work can be improved, and also based on the study findings, point out whether there are areas that deserve further investigation. This section will indicate whether a researcher has a firm appreciation of his/her work, and whether he /she has given sufficient thought to his appreciations, not only within the narrow confines of the research topic but to related fields. This section refracts the researcher's foresightedness and creativity.

Similarities of Proposal and Thesis /Project

1. The thesis must be prepared by typing it using the font size 12-point typeface of Times New Roman or Arial 12-point type face. It should be double spaced and printed on one side of the paper.
2. A 50mm margin should be left on the left side of the paper and a 25mm on the right side margin of the paper. Typing should begin 40mm from the top of the paper and should not go beyond 25mm from the bottom of the page.
3. All reference must be complete and consistently applied in the format indicated in chapter 7.
4. All figures must produced using a computer graphics package and have figure number and title.

5. *Gender specific words should be avoided. Words like author, researcher, and engineer, for example, should be used instead of 'he' or 'she'.*

6. *Pagination: The preliminaries (title page, declarations and abbreviations) Should be numbered in roman numerals lower cases e.g. i ii iii..........*

7. *The text, chapter 1 to appendices should be numbered using Arabic numerals. The number should appear in the center of the upper margin of the page.*

8. *Language used. In writing thesis, past tense should be used. This is mainly because the author is reporting what has already been carried out and completed.*

9. *Location of the research study should be the same in both proposal and thesis.*

CHAPTER THREE

DATA ANALYSIS PROCEDURES

3.0 Introduction

Data analysis refers to examining all that has been collected in a research study in order to making some deductions and inferences. It involves uncovering underlying structures; extracting important variables, detecting any an unusual behavior in the data and testing any assumptions. The researcher scrutinizes the collected information and makes some inferences. Statistical data analysis divides the methods for analyzing data into two categories: exploratory methods and confirmatory methods, (Kombo and Tromp, 2006). Exploratory methods are used to discover what the data seems to be saying and this is summarized by use of simple mathematical methods and simple representative diagrams. Confirmatory methods use ideas from probability theory to attempt to answer the specific questions. The two methods discussed are mainly applicable in quantitative research. As discussed in the Lecture on Research designs and Methodologies, the methods used in data analysis are influenced by whether the research is qualitative or quantitative or both. But whether both or not, the methods of analysis do not vary significantly

3.1 Importance of data analysis

In data analysis, the analyst breaks down data into constituents' parts to obtain answers to research questions or problem statements and in order to test the research hypotheses.
In qualitative research, data can be analyzed by a quick summary that will involves summarizing key findings through focusing in group discussions. In this kind of process, the researcher notes down the frequent responses of the participants on various issues. The said quick summary of qualitative data also involves explanations, interpretations and conclusion.

This rapid data analysis technique is mainly used in situations that require urgent information to make decisions for a program. For example, in place where there is an outbreak of such as ailments as cholera and vital information is need for intervention. This technique can also be used when the results already generated are obvious, making further analysis of data unwarranted. By obvious, it is implied that if a researcher finds out that over 75% of respondent give similar answers to what caused a cholera outbreak, doing further analysis may be unnecessary. This form of analysis does not require data transcription. The researcher records key issues of the discussion with respondents. A **narrative report** is written enriched with quotations from key informants and other respondents.

In and of itself, the analysis of research data does not provide the required answers. Interpretation of the data is very important and a necessary condition for answers to be arrived at. Interpretation means explaining to find the meaning. To explain raw data is difficult or impossible. It requires expertise in data manipulations which includes

24

interpretation in order to arrive at the meaning. For example, in quantitative research, data analysis consists of measurements in numerical values from which descriptions such as **mean, mode, range and standard deviations** are made. These data can be put into some order and further divided into two groups: *discrete data* or *continuous data*. Discrete data are countable data, e.g. the number of notable items produced during a day's production. Continuous data are parameters (variables) that are measured and are expressed on a continuous scale, e.g. the height of a person. The analysis of quantitative data varies from simple to more elaborate analysis techniques. The analysis varies with the objectives of the experiment, its complexity and the extent to which conclusion can be easily reached. Data analysis in quantitative research depends on the type of study such as: Correlation study, Prediction study, Causal-comparative research etc. The research analyst breaks down data into constituent parts to obtain answers to research questions (problem statements) and to test research hypotheses.

It is only after the interpretation of analyzed data that answers to problem questions are arrived at. Therefore we have to analyze the data first and then explain the result. That is, interpret the results of the analysis done. All we are saying is that, we have to categorize the data, order the data, manipulate the data and summarize the data to obtain answers to the questions. So, it means that the purpose of analysis is to reduce the data to intelligible and interpretable form so that the relations of research problems can be studied and tested.

To do all this we need to make use of statistics since the primary purpose of statistics in research is to manipulate and summarize the numerical data and the results obtained, compared with chance expectations. That is, the researcher must have hypothesized that styles of leadership affect group participation in certain ways. The researcher plans an experiment, executes the plan, and gathers data from the subjects. If the research question is: "How do styles of leadership affect group-member participation?" the researcher must put down analysis paradigms or models even when working on the problem and hypotheses.

The interpretation takes the results of analysis, makes inferences pertinent to research relations studied, and draws conclusions about the relations, searching for their meaning and implications, (Kerlinger, 2004). There are many kinds of statistical analysis and presentations available and we cannot discuss them all in details here.

3.2 Procedures in Data Analysis

MadhuBala, of Indira Gandhi National Open University,(2005) discussed the

following process for data analysis.

"Once you have selected the topic of the research and have gone through the process of literature survey, established your own focus of research, selected the research paradigm and methodology, prepared your own research plan and have collected the data; the next step is analysis of the data collected, before finally writing the research report.

- o Data analysis is an ongoing activity, which not only answers your question but also gives you the directions for future data collection. Data analysis procedures (DAP) help you to arrive at the data analysis. The uses of such procedures put your research project in perspective and assist you in testing the hypotheses with which you have started your research. Hence with the use of DAP, you can:-
- convert data into information and knowledge, and
- explore the relationship between variables.
  - o Understanding of the data analysis procedures will help you to
- appreciate the meaning of the scientific method, hypotheses testing and statistical significance in relation to research questions
- realise the importance of good research design when investigating research questions
- have knowledge of a range of inferential statistics and their applicability and limitations in the context of your research
- be able to devise, implement and report accurately a small quantitative research project
- be capable of identifying the data analysis procedures relevant to your research project
- show an understanding of the strengths and limitations of the selected quantitative and/or qualitative research project
- demonstrate the ability to use word processing, project planning and statistical computer packages in the context of a quantitative research project and report
- be adept of working effectively alone or with others to solve a research question/ problem quantitatively.

The literature survey which you carried out guides you through the various data analysis methods that have been used in similar studies. Depending upon your research paradigm and methodology and the type of data collection, this also assists you in data analysis. Hence once you are aware of the fact that which particular procedure is relevant to your research project, you get the answers to:

- What kinds of data analysis tools are identified for similar research investigations? and
- What data analysis procedures should you use for your purpose?
  - o There are numerous ways under which data analysis procedures are broadly defined. The following diagram, FigA3 makes it clear.

26

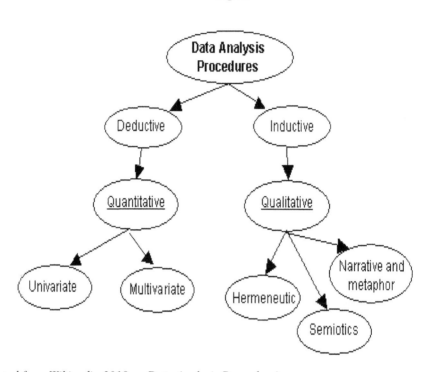

(Adopted from Wikipedia-2010 on Data Analysis Procedure)

There are, in fact, a number of software packages available that facilitate data analysis. These include statistical packages like SPSS, SAS, and Microsoft Excel etc. Similarly tools like spreadsheets and word processing software are multipurpose and very useful for data analysis. Apart from data analysis procedures, there is another factor which is secondary analysis of qualitative data.

People generally believe in the universal notion that "one can prove anything with statistics." This is only true if we use data analysis procedures improperly. There are some points that people often overlook while doing data analysis, and also the way(s) people sometimes "bend the rules" of statistics to support their viewpoint. The following website discusses them very clearly. Taking examples from medicine, education, and industry, it discusses the different ways in which you can make sure that your own statistical procedures are clear and accurate.

Since data analysis involves uncovering the structures underlying it, (Kombo and Tromp,2006), it means that extracting important information, variables and detecting any anomalies will help very much in testing the underlying assumptions, thus giving the analysis a meaningful interpretation.

There are two major methods of statistical data analysis: exploratory and confirmatory methods. Exploratory is mostly used in qualitative research while Confirmatory methods use probabilistic ideas. Based on the theory of probability, confirmatory methods attempt to answer specific questions. Confirmatory methods are usually applicable in quantitative research. From the above explanation, we can see that data analysis methods are influenced by the type of research design we have. That is, whether it is quantitative, qualitative or both.

In Qualitative data analysis, for example where we have to find out the views of people regarding certain issues pertaining to increased rate of suicide among young people, or increased rate of abortion among the youth, such findings are not always computable by arithmetic relations. The responses are only categorizable into various classes some of which are descriptive analysis.

3.3 Analysis of Qualitative Data

Qualitative data is often organized into categories to some extent but the categories are analyzed for their meaning and, often for their unique qualities and insights provided. Analogies are employed as in early investigative work in any science.

Validity, for qualitative researchers, is established through several means:

- The naturalistic and realistic nature of the data obtained

- Triangulation –use of several perspectives

- The fact that the research cycle is repeated; participants are re-interviewed and early hunches followed up further for instance

- Consultation and rapport with participants reducing their wariness, reticence, or need to obscure true opinions and thinking.

> Qualitative data consists of any information, gathered during research which has not (yet, at least) been quantified in any rigorous way.

3.4 Qualitative Data and Hypotheses' Testing

Because of the over-powering paradigm of natural science, it is often assumed that hypotheses can only be tested with quantified, empirical data. But we use qualitative data very often in supporting and contradicting our predictions and explanations.

Much of our reasoning about people's motivations and decision making is based on qualitative evidence. We may explain the unusual or depressive behavior of a friend in terms of her unique situation being a single parent and having just lost a supportive parent.

We can predict that persistent young offenders will feel more alienated from middle class society. We can demonstrate this with the sheer strength and animosity of the content of their accounts. We are not limited to simply counting the number of aggressive responses. No doubt it will be argued that 'strength and animosity' must come from comparison with other accounts, but what informs us here are the qualitative differences in content.

The positivism may well feel tempted to create a standardized questionnaire from the offenders elsewhere, or on a control group.

The point being made, however, is that some psychological researchers have argued forcefully for the need to use the qualitative content gained in their research. It is un expected meaning contained in offenders' account which will be of use, not the trivial but true fact that their accounts will somehow differ from non-offenders' accounts. It is what offenders say, and we may never have heard, which research uncovers and highlights for debate. The qualitative researchers might argue too, that insights gained in interviewing a group of offenders can be generalized with as much validity as questionnaire results. A perspective on the world, quite novel and unexpected, may emerge from the interview and give another interviewer a new range of ideas to broach with different offenders, or with 'control' teenagers who don't share the ideas. We have seen elsewhere that individual case studies can add important information to the pool of knowledge and ideas which constitutes our understanding of human and their behaviors. The value of Watson's study of 'little Albert' was not that it was entirely quantitative. In a single subject study we learnt just how easy it was to conditions a child's fear and we acquired interesting information about how these generalized and failed to extinguish. It seems a bit futile to argue that we should compare with a control child to ensure that the stage Albert went through did not occur just by chance. There is extremely valuable qualitative information contained within many reports or even traditionally organized research. The interviews with Asch's participants, post testing, are illuminating and it was necessary to ask Milgram's participants why they seemed to chuckle as they the thought they delivered fatal electric shock to an innocent victim. The extent of their stress, which forced this nervous laughter, is far more readily got at through the interview process and discussion of the meaning of what participants said.

3.5 Two Approaches to Qualitative Data

Looking through the literature on qualitative data, two general views seem to emerge on what to do with it. These correspond to the positivist non-positivist dimension but it must be stressed that this is a dimension – there are not just two views but a wide variety. For the positivist, unquantified data is accepted in a subsidiary role. It is seen as having the following uses:

- It can illustrate and give a context to otherwise neutral and uninspiring statistics, as when Asch tells us how his conforming participants behaved and looked uncomfortable.

- It can lead us to hypotheses testable in quantitative terms, as with the children of unemployed parents.

The qualitative researcher, however, sees qualitative data as meaningful in its own right. In fact, the use of the term 'qualitative method' usually indicates a commitment to publish the results of research in qualitative terms, remembering, of course, that such a researcher is not averse to looking things qualitatively, should be opportunity arise and be found illuminating.

3.6 Methods of Analysis

It is not possible to give precise guidelines on the analysis and presentation of qualitative data. There is no universally accepted paradigm. The decisions will be influenced by the theoretical background or model from which the researcher is working. Several quite specialized methods of analysis have been developed for different sorts of data. (Conversations, non-verbal communication, pedestrian behavior and so on). What follows is a set of points applying to collections of data produced from the types of source mentioned above. After that the reader will be directed to several specialized texts which have more to say on various qualitative or 'new paradigm' methods.

3.7 Reliability and Validity in Qualitative Research

Qualitative researchers argue that their methods produce more valid data for reasons already discussed. They would also argue that they have developed safeguards against lack of reliability. Some of these follow:
- *Triangulation*

Borrowed from surveying, and used in evaluative research, this means comparing two different views of the same thing; interview with observational data, open with closed questions or one researchers' analysis with one another's.
- *Analysis of negative cases*

This is consideration of why certain cases just don't fit the major patterns outlined as results of analysis. The willingness to do this openly is held to be a validity check. Others can accept the proffered explanation or not, and can call for reanalysis, analyses raw data themselves or attempt some form of replication.
- *Repetition of the research cycle*

Qualitative researchers go round the 'research cycle' several times. The researcher checks and rechecks the early assumptions and inferences made. As patterns and theories are developed, so the researcher goes back in again to gather more information which should confirm tentative hypotheses and/or help to further refine, deepen and clarify categories.
- *Participant consultation*

Participants are consulted and provide feedback. Qualitative researchers 'at the non-alienating end of the (research) spectrum' (Reason, 1981) involve the participants in evaluation of tentative conclusions and refine these in the light of feedback from these process. Reason makes the point; "Once the start to do research which does not conform to the general requirements of experimental methods, we run the risk of being accused of being mere journalist; Indeed we run the risk of being merely journalists."

Reason's answer to this criticism is an eloquent argument summarized in these last two safeguards. Journalists, he argues tend to one round, depart and write fairly impressionistic accounts, with little, if any, feedback process.

In Quantitative data analysis the procedures consist of measuring of numerical values, (Kombo and Tromp, 2006) where measures of central tendency, measures of variability are worked out and various inferences done. These numerical data can be either discrete or continuous, meaning either countable data or parametric (variables), measurable and expressed on a continuous scale, for example, the height of a person. Quantitative data analysis varies from simple to complex due to differences in , especially experiments done for the purpose of data collection.

In correlation research studies data is mainly analyzed using some kind of coefficient of correlation. This implies the degree of relationship between variables, usually two variables. The degree of relationship varies from (positive 1), perfect correlation; no correlation (zero) to (negative 1), perfect opposite correlation.

Although there are still more types of correlation analysis such as reliability and validity studies that require our mention here, we may not be able to go through them now until later when we discuss exhaustively the concepts of validity and reliability of data, what constitutes validity and reliability in research studies.

3.8 Summary

The methods used in data analysis are influenced by whether the research is qualitative or quantitative or both. But whether both or not, the methods of analysis do not vary significantly. To explain raw data is difficult or impossible. It requires expertise in data manipulations which includes interpretation in order to arrive at the meaning. After interpretation of analyzed data then answers to problem questions are arrived at. The two major methods of statistical data analysis are exploratory and confirmatory. Exploratory is mostly used in qualitative research while Confirmatory methods use the theory of probability.

CHAPTER FOUR

SELECTION OF RESEARCH DESIGN METHODOLOGIES

4.0 Introduction

Research design is the plan, the structure and strategy of investigation conceived so as to obtain answers to research questions and to control variance, (Kerlinger, 2004). It is quite important for any researcher to have an idea what type of data he/she expects to collect and even how such information, (data) will be manipulated in order to come up with the expected finding of his research. The research questions or problem statements will be the best guide as to the appropriateness of the research design and the methodology the researcher will follow in the study. Research designs are used to enable the researcher answer questions as validly, objectively, accurately and economically as possible. Any research plan is deliberately and specifically conceived and executed to bring about empirical evidence to bear on the research problem. The researcher might find that instead of the study dictating only quantitative research design methodologies, some of its parts might also be calling up some qualitative design due to various techniques applied in data collection and manipulation. Or the researcher may find himself/herself using both methodologies (multi-method).

4.1 Research Design and Methodologies

An hypothesis is a logical supposition, a reasonable guess, or an educated conjecture on relationships between a factor and a phenomenon under investigation. It is formulated by the investigator on the basis of the problem or sub-problems of the research study. The importance of a hypothesis is that it guides the research activity. An investigator may refer to the hypothesis in directing his or her thought process toward the possible solution to the research problems or problem statements.

The researcher might want to identify the most frequently occurring type(s) of disruptive behavior in a particular classroom. With clear prior agreement on what constitutes such "disruptive behavior". Characterized by such interrogatives as "what is....?; what are.....?; identifying......; and exploratory type studies, the design process is to *"Identify" "what is* ("what are") the perceived behaviors that are disruptive. Note that this is a *Descriptive problem statement* and so it requires that *descriptive research design methodology*. Similarly, the researcher will use the various kinds of problem statements or research questions and come up with the type of research design methodology that will satisfactorily provide answers to the questions. Many of such research designs will include: *Survey* or *observational* research designs which are within the *Descriptive research designs methodologies*, or True experimental, Quasi-experimental or Ex-post facto which are in group *comparison research design* and could also be *Correlational research design methodology.*

4.2 Correlational Designs

Correlation Research Designs "link" to the keywords of "association," "relationship," and/or "predictive ability" that we've come to associate with "correlational" research questions or problem statements. Correlational design enables the researcher to assess the degree of relationship existing between two or more variables, (Orodho, 2003). For example, we can compare the performance in examinations of day-pupils and those who are boarders. Here we use a correlation design. But at times we cannot conclusively prove that the poor performance or good performance is related to either boarding or otherwise because there are other factors that influence either good or poor performance in examinations. But if careful control of other possible variables can be done, then we are able to find a causal relation.

Other types of research designs that may be useful in this study include:

i. **Case study design**: which seeks to describe exhaustively a unit of study. It is a way of organizing our data and looking at the way they can be studied as a whole. For example, *The impact of Free Primary Education on Child labor: A case study of Nyeri County in Kenya.* Such would bring about a deeper understanding of how children's rights to education are abused in the name of helping the poor children who cannot afford education fees.

ii. **Group Comparisons**: Tight control (the researcher attempts to identify in advance as many possible 'contaminating' and/or confounding variables as possible and to control for them in his/her design -- by, say, building them in and balancing on them, e.g. equal numbers of boys and girls to 'control for gender' or 'randomizing them away' by drawing a random sample of subjects and thereby 'getting a good mix' on them, e.g., all levels of 'socioeconomic status') Because of the preceding control, the 'confidence' to make 'cause/effect statements' That is, we begin to get the idea of 2 or more groups, as balanced and equivalent as possible on all but one "thing:" our "treatment" (e.g., type of lesson, type of counseling). We measure them before and after this treatment and if we do find a difference in the group that 'got the treatment,' we hope to attribute that difference to the treatment only (because of this tight control, randomization, and so forth).

iii) Cross Cultural research design
This design is used to study behavior patterns of different cultures. Through such a design we are able to get deeper understanding of how different cultures behave under similar circumstances. For example comparing the educational performance pupils in rural schools and those in urban schools.

In Selecting a research design it is important to follow some basic guidelines:
   a) What kind of a research one intends to do. That is the purpose and objectives of one's   study will guide as to which design one is going to select.
   b) Use of text books and journals written on the topic of your intended research study will   equally give further clarification as to what design will suit your study

c) Consulting with other professionals will also guide your selection of the kind of research design you will use. It is through such consultations that one gets the validity and or reliability of one's research study and come up with a decision as to what kind of design one will use. For example, in quantitative research design, other than thinking of only numerical data involvement, there are a lot of other activities that precede and follow the central idea of numerical/statistical work. Let us look at it here.

4.3 Quantitative research

In the social sciences, **quantitative research** refers to the systematic empirical investigation of social phenomena via statistical, mathematical or computational techniques. The objective of quantitative research is to develop and employ mathematical models, theories and/or hypothesis pertaining to phenomena. The process of measurement is central to quantitative research because it provides the fundamental connection between empirical observation and mathematical expression of quantitative relationships. Quantitative data is any data that is in numerical form such as statistics, percentages, etc. In layman's terms, this means that the quantitative researcher asks a specific, narrow question and collects numerical data from participants to answer the question. The researcher analyzes the data with the help of statistics. The researcher is hoping the numbers will yield an unbiased result that can be generalized to some larger population. Qualitative research, on the other hand, asks broad questions and collects word data from participants. The researcher looks for themes and describes the information in themes and patterns exclusive to that set of participants.

Quantitative research is used widely in social sciences such as psychology, economics, sociology, and political science, and less frequently in anthropology and history. Research in mathematical sciences such as physics is also 'quantitative' by definition, though this use of the term differs in context. In the social sciences, the term relates to empirical methods, originating in both philosophical positivism and the history of statistics, which contrast qualitative research methods.

Qualitative methods produce information only on the particular cases studied, and any more general conclusions are only hypotheses. Quantitative methods can be used to verify which of such hypotheses are true.

A comprehensive analysis of 1274 articles published in the top two American sociology journals between 1935 and 2005 found that roughly two thirds of these articles used quantitative methods. Quantitative research is generally made using scientific methods, which can include:

- The generation of models, theories and hypothesis
- The development of instruments and methods for measurement
- Experimental control and manipulation of variables
- Collection of empirical data
- Modeling and analysis of data

34

In the social sciences particularly, quantitative research is often contrasted with qualitative research which is the examination, analysis and interpretation of observations for the purpose of discovering underlying meanings and patterns of relationships, including classifications of types of phenomena and entities, in a manner that does not involve mathematical models. Approaches to quantitative psychology were first modeled on quantitative approaches in the physical sciences by Gustav Fechner in his work on psychophysics, which built on the work of Ernst Heinrich Weber. Although a distinction is commonly drawn between qualitative and quantitative aspects of scientific investigation, it has been argued that the two go hand in hand. For example, based on analysis of the history of science, Kuhn (1961) concludes that "large amounts of qualitative work have usually been prerequisite to fruitful quantification in the physical sciences". Qualitative research is often used to gain a general sense of phenomena and to form theories that can be tested using further quantitative research. For instance, in the social sciences qualitative research methods are often used to gain better understanding of such things as intentionality (from the speech response of the researchee) and meaning (why did this person/group say something and what did it mean to them?) (Kieron Yeoman).

Although quantitative investigation of the world has existed since people first began to record events or objects that had been counted, the modern idea of quantitative processes have their roots in Auguste Comte's positivist framework. Positivism emphasized the use of the scientific method through observation to empirically test hypotheses explaining and predicting what, where, why, how, and when phenomena occurred. Positivist scholars like Comte believed only scientific methods rather than previous spiritual explanations for human behavior could advance science.

4.4 Use of Statistics

Statistics is the most widely used branch of mathematics in quantitative research outside of the physical sciences, and also finds applications within the physical sciences, such as in statistical mechanics. Statistical methods are used extensively within fields such as economics, social sciences and biology. Quantitative research using statistical methods starts with the collection of data, based on the hypothesis or theory. Usually a big sample of data is collected - this would require verification, validation and recording before the analysis can take place. Software packages such as SPSS and R are typically used for this purpose. Causal relationships are studied by manipulating factors thought to influence the phenomena of interest while controlling other variables relevant to the experimental outcomes. In the field of health, for example, researchers might measure and study the relationship between dietary intake and measurable physiological effects such as weight loss, controlling for other key variables such as exercise. Quantitatively based opinion surveys are widely used in the media, with statistics such as the proportion of respondents in favor of a position commonly reported. In opinion surveys, respondents are asked a set of structured questions and their responses are tabulated. In the field of climate science, researchers compile and compare statistics such as temperature or atmospheric concentrations of carbon dioxide.

Empirical relationships and associations are also frequently studied by using some form of General linear model, non-linear model, or by using factor analysis. A fundamental principle in quantitative research is that correlation does not imply causation, although some such as Clive

Granger suggest that a series of correlations can imply a degree of causality. This principle follows from the fact that it is always possible a spurious relationship exists for variables between which covariance is found in some degree. Associations may be examined between any combination of continuous and categorical variables using methods of statistics.

4.5 Measurement

Views regarding the role of measurement in quantitative research are somewhat divergent. Measurement is often regarded as being only a means by which observations are expressed numerically in order to investigate causal relations or associations. However, it has been argued that measurement often plays a more important role in quantitative research. For example, Kuhn argued that within quantitative research, the results that are shown can prove to be strange. This is because accepting a theory based on results of quantitative data could prove to be a natural phenomenon. He argued that such abnormalities are interesting when done during the process of obtaining data, as seen below:

When measurement departs from theory, it is likely to yield mere numbers, and their very neutrality makes them particularly sterile as a source of remedial suggestions. But numbers register the departure from theory with an authority and finesse that no qualitative technique can duplicate, and that departure is often enough to start a search (Kuhn, 1961, p. 180). In classical physics, the theory and definitions which underpin measurement are generally deterministic in nature. In contrast, probabilistic measurement models known as the Rasch model and Item response theory models are generally employed in the social sciences. Psychometrics is the field of study concerned with the theory and technique for measuring social and psychological attributes and phenomena. This field is central to much quantitative research that is undertaken within the social sciences.

Quantitative research may involve the use of *proxies* as stand-ins for other quantities that cannot be directly measured. Tree-ring width, for example, is considered a reliable proxy of ambient environmental conditions such as the warmth of growing seasons or amount of rainfall. Although scientists cannot directly measure the temperature of past years, tree-ring width and other climate proxies have been used to provide a semi-quantitative record of average temperature in the Northern Hemisphere back to 1000 A.D. When used in this way, the proxy record (tree ring width, say) only reconstructs a certain amount of the variance of the original record. The proxy may be calibrated (for example, during the period of the instrumental record) to determine how much variation is captured, including whether both short and long term variation is revealed. In the case of tree-ring width, different species in different places may show more or less sensitivity to, say, rainfall or temperature: when reconstructing a temperature record there is considerable skill in selecting proxies that are well correlated with the desired variable.

4.6 Relationship with Qualitative Methods

In most physical and biological sciences, the use of either quantitative or qualitative methods is uncontroversial, and each is used when appropriate. In the social sciences, particularly in sociology, social anthropology and psychology, the use of one or other type of method can be a matter of controversy and even ideology, with particular schools of thought within each discipline favoring one type of method and pouring scorn on to the other. The majority tendency throughout the history of social science, however, is to use eclectic approaches-by combining both methods. Qualitative methods might be used to understand the meaning of the conclusions produced by quantitative methods. Using quantitative methods, it is possible to give precise and testable expression to qualitative ideas. This combination of quantitative and qualitative data gathering is often referred to as mixed-methods research.

Examples

- Research that consists of the percentage amounts of all the elements that make up Earth's atmosphere.
- Survey that concludes that the average patient has to wait two hours in the waiting room of a certain doctor before being selected.
- An experiment in which group x was given two tablets of Aspirin a day and Group y was given two tablets of a placebo a day where each participant is randomly assigned to one or other of the groups. The numerical factors such as two tablets, percent of elements and the time of waiting make the situations and results quantitative.
- In finance, quantitative research into the stock markets is used to develop models to price complex trades, and develop algorithms to exploit investment hypotheses

In **quantitative research design** your aim is to determine the relationship between one thing (an independent variable) and another (a dependent or outcome variable) in a population. Quantitative research designs are either descriptive (subjects usually measured once) or experimental (subjects measured before and after a treatment). A descriptive study establishes only associations between variables. An experiment establishes causality. For an accurate estimate of the relationship between variables, a descriptive study usually needs a sample of hundreds or even thousands of subjects; an experiment, especially a crossover, may need only tens of subjects. The estimate of the relationship is less likely to be biased if you have a high participation rate in a sample selected randomly from a population. In experiments, bias is also less likely if subjects are randomly assigned to treatments, and if subjects and researchers are blind to the identity of the treatments.

In all studies, subject characteristics can affect the relationship you are investigating. Limit their effect either by using a less heterogeneous sample of subjects or preferably by measuring the characteristics and including them in the analysis. In an experiment, try to measure variables that might explain the mechanism of the treatment.

Studies aimed at quantifying relationships are of two types: **descriptive or observational** and **experimental**. In a descriptive study, no attempt is made to change behavior or conditions--you measure things as they are. In an experimental study you take measurements, try some sort of intervention, then take measurements again to see what happened.

In Descriptive or Observational we have the following designs:

- case

- case series
- cross-sectional
- cohort or prospective or longitudinal
- case-control or retrospective

In Experimental, longitudinal or repeated-measures we have:

- without a control group,
- with a control group

4.7 Descriptive Studies

Descriptive studies are also called **observational**, because you observe the subjects without otherwise intervening. The simplest descriptive study is a **case**, which reports data on only one subject; examples are a study of an outstanding athlete or of a dysfunctional institution. Descriptive studies of a few cases are called **case series**. In **cross-sectional** studies variables of interest in a sample of subjects are assayed once and the relationships between them are determined. In **prospective** or **cohort** studies, some variables are assayed at the start of a study (e.g., dietary habits), then after a period of time the outcomes are determined (e.g., incidence of heart disease). Another label for this kind of study is **longitudinal**, although this term also applies to experiments. **Case-control** studies compare **cases** (subjects with a particular attribute, such as an injury or ability) with **controls** (subjects without the attribute); comparison is made of the **exposure** to something suspected of causing the cases, for example volume of high intensity training, or number of alcoholic drinks consumed per day. Case-control studies are also called **retrospective**, because they focus on conditions in the past that might have caused subjects to become cases rather than controls.

A common case-control design in the exercise science literature is a comparison of the behavioral, psychological or anthropometric characteristics of elite and sub-elite athletes: you are interested in what the elite athletes have been exposed to that makes them better than the sub-elites. Another type of study compares athletes with sedentary people on some outcome such as an injury, disease, or disease risk factor. Here you know the difference in exposure (training vs no training), so these studies are really cohort or prospective, even though the exposure data are gathered retrospectively at only one time point. The technical name for these studies is **historical cohort**.

4.8 Experimental Studies

- Experimental studies are also known as **longitudinal** or **repeated-measures** studies, for obvious reasons. They are also referred to as **interventions**, because you do more than just observe the subjects.
- In the simplest experiment, a **time series**, one or more measurements are taken on all subjects before and after a treatment. A special case of the time series is the so-called **single-subject design**, in which measurements are taken repeatedly (e.g., 10 times) before and after an intervention on one or a few subjects.

38

- Time series suffer from a major problem: any change you see could be due to something other than the treatment. For example, subjects might do better on the second test because of their experience of the first test, or they might change their diet between tests because of a change in weather, and diet could affect their performance of the test. The **crossover** design is one solution to this problem. Normally the subjects are given two treatments, one being the real treatment, the other a control or reference treatment. Half the subjects receive the real treatment first, the other half the control first. After a period of time sufficient to allow any treatment effect to wash out, the treatments are crossed over. Any effect of retesting or of anything that happened between the tests can then be subtracted out by an appropriate analysis. **Multiple crossover** designs involving several treatments are also possible.
- If the treatment effect is unlikely to wash out between measurements, a **control group** has to be used. In these designs, all subjects are measured, but only some of them--the **experimental group**--then receive the treatment. All subjects are then measured again, and the change in the experimental group is compared with the change in the control group.
- If the subjects are assigned randomly to experimental and control groups or treatments, the design is known as a **randomized controlled trial**. Random assignment minimizes the chance that either group is not typical of the population. If the subjects are **blind** (or **masked**) to the identity of the treatment, the design is a **single-blind** controlled trial. The control or reference treatment in such a study is called a **placebo**: the name physicians use for inactive pills or treatments that are given to patients in the guise of effective treatments. Blinding of subjects eliminates the **placebo effect**, whereby people react differently to a treatment if they think it is in some way special. In a **double-blind** study, the experimenter also does not know which treatment the subjects receive until all measurements are taken. Blinding of the experimenter is important to stop him or her treating subjects in one group differently from those in another. In the best studies even the data are analyzed blind, to prevent conscious or unconscious fudging or prejudiced interpretation.
- Ethical considerations or lack of cooperation (compliance) by the subjects sometimes prevent experiments from being performed. For example, a randomized controlled trial of the effects of physical activity on heart disease may not have been performed yet, because it is unethical and unrealistic to randomize people to 10 years of exercise or sloth. But there have been many short-term studies of the effects of physical activity on disease risk factors (e.g., blood pressure).

4.9 Quality of Designs

The various designs differ in the quality of evidence they provide for a cause-and-effect relationship between variables. Cases and case series are the weakest. A well-designed cross-sectional or case-control study can provide good evidence for the **absence** of a relationship. But if such a study does reveal a relationship, it generally represents only suggestive evidence of a causal connection. A cross-sectional or case-control study is therefore a good starting point to decide whether it is worth proceeding to better designs. Prospective studies are more difficult and time-consuming to perform, but they produce more convincing conclusions about cause and effect. Experimental studies provide the best evidence about how something affects something else, and double-blind randomized controlled trials are the best experiments.

Confounding is a potential problem in descriptive studies that try to establish cause and effect. Confounding occurs when part or all of a significant association between two variables arises through both being causally associated with a third variable. For example, in a population study you could easily show a negative association between habitual activity and most forms of degenerative disease. But older people are less active, and older people are more diseased, so you're bound to find an association between activity and disease without one necessarily causing the other. To get over this problem you have to **control for potential confounding factors**. For example, you make sure all your subjects are the same age, or you include age in the analysis to try to remove its effect on the relationship between the other two variables.

4.9.1 Samples

You almost always have to work with a **sample** of subjects rather than the full **population**. But people are interested in the population, not your sample. To **generalize** from the sample to the population, the sample has to be **representative** of the population. The safest way to ensure that it is representative is to use a **random** selection procedure. You can also use a **stratified** random sampling procedure, to make sure that you have proportional representation of population subgroups (e.g., sexes, races, regions).

When the sample is not representative of the population, **selection bias** is a possibility. A statistic is biased if the value of the statistic tends to be wrong (or more precisely, if the expected value--the average value from many samples drawn using the same sampling method--is not the same as the population value.) A typical source of bias in population studies is age or socioeconomic status: people with extreme values for these variables tend not to take part in the studies. Thus a high **compliance** (the proportion of people contacted who end up as subjects) is important in avoiding bias. Journal editors are usually happy with compliance rates of at least 70%.

Failure to randomize subjects to control and treatment groups in experiments can also produce bias. If you let people select themselves into the groups, or if you select the groups in any way that makes one group different from another, then any result you get might reflect the group difference rather than an effect of the treatment. For this reason, it's important to randomly assign subjects in a way that ensures the groups are **balanced** in terms of important variables that could modify the effect of the treatment (e.g., age, gender, physical performance). Human subjects may not be happy about being randomized, so you need to state clearly that it is a condition of taking part.

Often the most important variable to balance is the pre-test value of the dependent variable itself. You can get close to perfectly balanced randomization for this or another numeric variable as follows: rank-order the subjects on the value of the variable; split the list up into pairs (or triplets for three treatments, etc.); assign the lowest ranked subject to a treatment by flipping a coin; assign the next two subjects (the other member of the pair, and the first member of the next pair) to the other treatment; assign the next two subjects to the first treatment, and so on. If you have male and female subjects, or any other grouping that you think might affect the treatment, perform this randomization process for each group ranked separately. Data from such pair-matched studies can be analyzed in ways that may increase the precision of the estimate of the treatment effect. Watch this space for an update shortly. When selecting subjects and designing protocols for experiments, researchers often strive to eliminate all variation in subject characteristics and behaviors. Their aim is to get greater precision in the estimate of the effect of the treatment. The problem with this approach is that the effect generalizes only to subjects with the same narrow range of characteristics and behaviors as in the sample. Depending on the nature of the study, you may therefore have to strike a balance between precision and applicability. If you lean towards applicability, your subjects will vary substantially on some characteristic or behavior that you should measure and include in your analysis.

4.9.2 Sample Size

How many subjects should you study? You can approach this crucial issue via statistical significance, confidence intervals, or "on the fly".

4.9.3 Via Statistical Significance

Statistical significance is the standard but somewhat complicated approach. Your sample size has to be big enough for you to be sure you will detect the smallest worthwhile effect or relationship between your variables. *To be sure* means detecting the effect 80% of the time. *Detect* means getting a statistically significant effect, which means that more than 95% of the time you'd expect to see a value for the effect numerically smaller than what you observed, if there was no effect at all in the population (in other words, the p value for the effect has to be less than 0.05). *Smallest worthwhile effect* means the smallest effect that would make a difference to the lives of your subjects or to your interpretation of whatever you are studying. If you have too few subjects in your study and you get a statistically significant effect, most people regard your finding as publishable. But if the effect is not significant with a small sample size, most people regard it (erroneously) as unpublishable.

4.9.4 Via Confidence Intervals

Using confidence intervals or confidence limits is a more accessible approach to sample-size estimation and interpretation of outcomes. You simply want enough subjects to give acceptable precision for the effect you are studying. *Precision* refers usually to a 95% confidence interval for the true value of the effect: the range within which the true (population) value for the effect is 95% likely to fall. *Acceptable* means it won't matter to your subjects (or to your interpretation of whatever you are studying) if the true value of the effect is as large as the upper limit or as small as the lower limit. A bonus of using confidence intervals to justify your choice of sample size is that the sample size is about half what you need if you use statistical significance.

"On the Fly"

An acceptable width for the confidence interval depends on the magnitude of the observed effect. If the observed effect is close to zero, the confidence interval has to be narrow, to exclude the possibility that the true (population) value could be substantially positive or substantially negative. If the observed effect is large, the confidence interval can be wider, because the true value of the effect is still large at either end of the confidence interval. I therefore recommend getting your sample size on the fly: start a study with a small sample size, then increase the number of subjects until you get a confidence interval that is appropriate for the magnitude of the effect that you end up with. I have run simulations to show the resulting magnitudes of effects are not substantially biased.

4.9.5 Effect of Research Design

The type of design you choose for your study has a major impact on the sample size. Descriptive studies need hundreds of subjects to give acceptable confidence intervals (or to ensure statistical significance) for small effects. Experiments generally need a lot less--often one-tenth as many-- because it's easier to see changes within subjects than differences between groups of subjects. Crossovers need even less--one-quarter of the number for an equivalent trial with a control group--because every subject gets the experimental treatment. I give details on the stats pages at this site.

4.9.6 Effect of Validity and Reliability

The precision with which you measure things also has a major impact on sample size: the worse your measurements, the more subjects you need to lift the signal (the effect) out of the noise (the errors in measurement). Precision is expressed as **validity** and **reliability**. Validity represents how well a variable measures what it is supposed to. Validity is important in descriptive studies: if the validity of the main variables is poor, you may need thousands rather than hundreds of subjects. Reliability tells you how reproducible your measures are on a retest, so it impacts experimental studies: the more reliable a measure, the less subjects you need to see a small change in the measure. For example, a controlled trial with 20 subjects in each group or a crossover with 10 subjects may be sufficient to characterize even a small effect, if the measure is highly reliable. See the details on the stats pages.

4.9.7 Pilot Studies

As a student researcher, you might not have enough time or resources to get a sample of optimum size. Your study can nevertheless be a **pilot** for a larger study. Perform a pilot study to develop, adapt, or check the feasibility of techniques, to determine the reliability of measures, and/or to calculate how big the final sample needs to be. In the latter case, the pilot should have the same sampling procedure and techniques as in the larger study.

For experimental designs, a pilot study can consist of the first 10 or so observations of a larger study. If you get respectable confidence limits, there may be no point in continuing to a larger sample. Publish and move on to the next project or lab!

If you can't test enough subjects to get an acceptably narrow confidence interval, you should still be able to publish your finding, because your study will set useful bounds on how big and how small the effect can be. A statistician can also combine your finding with the findings of similar studies in something called a **meta-analysis**, which derives a confidence interval for the effect from several studies. If your study is not published, it can't contribute to the meta-analysis! Many reviewers and editors do not appreciate this important point, because they are locked into thinking that only statistically significant results are publishable.

What to measure

In any study, you measure the **characteristics of the subjects**, and the **independent and dependent variables** defining the research question. For experiments, you can also measure **mechanism variables**, which help you explain how the treatment works.

4.9.8 Characteristics of Subjects

You must report sufficient information about your subjects to identify the population group from which they were drawn. For human subjects, variables such as sex, age, height, weight, socioeconomic status, and ethnic origin are common, depending on the focus of the study.

Show the ability of athletic subjects as current or personal-best performance, preferably expressed as a percent of world-record. For endurance athletes a direct or indirect estimate of maximum oxygen consumption helps characterize ability in a manner that is largely independent of the sport.

4.9.9 Dependent and Independent Variables

Usually you have a good idea of the question you want to answer. That question defines the main variables to measure. For example, if you are interested in enhancing sprint performance, your **dependent variable** (or **outcome** variable) is automatically some measure of sprint performance. Cast around for the way to measure this dependent variable with as much precision as possible.

Next, identify all the things that could affect the dependent variable. These things are the **independent variables**: training, sex, the treatment in an experimental study, and so on.

For a descriptive study with a wide focus (a "fishing expedition"), your main interest is estimating the effect of everything that is likely to affect the dependent variable, so you include as many independent variables as resources allow. For the large sample sizes that you should use in a descriptive study, including these variables does not lead to substantial loss of precision in the effect statistics, but beware: the more effects you look for, the more likely the true value of at least one of them lies outside its confidence interval (a problem I call cumulative Type 0 error). For a descriptive study with a narrower focus (e.g., the relationship between training and performance), you still measure variables likely to be associated with the outcome variable (e.g., age-group, sex, competitive status), because either you restrict the sample to a particular subgroup defined by these variables (e.g., veteran male elite athletes) or you include the variables in the analysis.

For an experimental study, the main independent variable is the one indicating when the dependent variable is measured (e.g., before, during, and after the treatment). If there is a control group (as in controlled trials) or control treatment (as in crossovers), the identity of the group or treatment is another essential independent variable (e.g., Drug A, Drug B, placebo in a controlled trial; drug-first and placebo-first in a crossover). These variables obviously have an affect on the dependent variable, so you automatically include them in any analysis.

Variables such as sex, age, diet, training status, and variables from blood or exercise tests can also affect the outcome in an experiment. For example, the response of males to the treatment might be different from that of females. Such variables account for **individual differences** in the response to the treatment, so it's important to take them into account. As for descriptive studies, either you restrict the study to one sex, one age, and so on, or you sample both sexes, various ages, and so on, then analyze the data with these variables included as **covariates**. I favor the latter approach, because it widens the applicability of your findings, but once again there is the problem of cumulative Type 0 error for the effect of these covariates. An additional problem with small sample sizes is loss of precision of the estimate of the effect, if you include more than two or three of these variables in the analysis.

4.10 Summary

We further focused in by talking about some important **components** of these research questions or problem statements: namely, variables and hypotheses. The design methodology (sometimes just called "design") consists of **the label(s) that characterize the "general blueprint" of the design**. Usually more than one design label apply to some particular studies. As with research questions or problem statements the form(s) of data that are collected will determine the design whether in numbers (quantitative), words (qualitative) or both (multi-method). Quantitative research is all about quantifying relationships between variables. Variables are things like weight, performance, time, and treatment. You measure variables on a sample of subjects, which can be tissues, cells, animals, or humans. You express the relationship between variable using effect statistics, such as correlations, relative frequencies, or differences between means. I deal with these statistics and other aspects of analysis elsewhere at this site. In this article I focus on the design of quantitative research. First I describe the types of study you can use. Next I discuss how the nature of the sample affects your ability to make statements about the relationship in the population. For an accurate estimate of the relationship between variables, a descriptive study usually needs a sample of hundreds or even thousands of subjects; an experiment, especially a crossover, may need only tens of subjects. The estimates of the relation- ship is less likely to be biased if you have a high participation rate in a sample selected randomly from a population. In experiments, bias is also less likely if subjects are randomly assigned to treatments, and if subjects and researchers are blind to the identity of the treatments. Statistics is the most widely used branch of mathematics in quantitative research outside of the physical sciences, and also finds applications within the physical sciences, such as in statistical mechanics. Statistical methods are used extensively within fields such as economics, social sciences and biology. Quantitative research using statistical methods starts with the collection of data, based on the hypothesis or theory.

CHAPTER FIVE

RESEARCH DESIGNS

5.0 Introduction

In order to come up with a well stated hypothesis, the concept of objectivity is very crucial. Objectivity is a characteristic of scientific research, which dictates that the procedures and subject matter of investigations should be such that they could, in principle, be agreed upon by everyone. In child psychology, the emphasis on objectivity is important because child psychology as a discipline focuses on observable behaviors. It is evident that in child psychology we have two primary goals:-to describe children's behavior at each point of their development and to find and identify the causes and processes that produce changes in behavior from one point to the next.

5.1 Analysis and Comparison of Research Designs

As we said earlier, a research design is a method, a plan, a structure or a strategy a researcher considers most appropriate to use to investigate research questions in his/her research study in order to come up with a solution(s) or an answer(s) to the research problem(s) or question(s) envisaged. That is, a Research Design is a plan so designed   as to offer the kind of route an Investigator has to follow and type of activities that will take place en-route in order to find a solution or solutions to identified problem(s). We can say, it is more than a plan, it is a strategy since it includes methods to be used to gather and analyze the data. In other words, strategy implies *how* the research objectives will be reached and *how* the problems encountered in research will be tackled. The investigator must put all these into consideration as thinks on the *research questions* or *problem statements* whose answers or solutions are being looked for.
Research design has two basic purposes:
- To provide answers to research questions
- To control variance.

Naturally, research design does not do these things. Only the investigator does. Design helps the investigator obtain answers to the questions of research and also helps him to control the experimental, extraneous, and error variances of the particular research problem under study. Since all research activity can be said to have the purpose of providing answers to research questions, it is possible to omit this purpose from the discussion and to say that research design has one grand purpose: *to control variance.* Such a delimitation of the purpose of design, however, is dangerous. Without strong stress on the research questions and on the use of design to help provide answers to these questions, the study of design can degenerate into an interesting, but sterile, technical exercise.
Research designs are intended to enable the researcher to answer research questions as validly, objectively, accurately, and economically as possible. Any research plan is deliberately and specifically thought of, and executed to bring about empirical evidence on the research problem. Research problems can be and are stated in the form of hypotheses. At times in the research, these problems are stated so that they can be empirically tested.
Below is a diagrammatic representation of *design methodologies* that could be used to any or all

46

of the three (3) major research designs as represented in Wikipedia (2010): - Qualitative, Quantitative or Multi-method.

Diagrammatic representation of Families of Research Designs

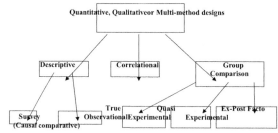

Descriptive Designs

Earlier we saw that descriptive designs link to descriptive questions or statements characterized by such interrogatives as "what is…?; What are…..?; identifying……; and exploratory type studies.

For Example:

This study is to *identify* the perceived barriers to a successful implementation of Early Childhood Development Education Programs in public primary schools in the past two decades in Kenya. The design process is to "Identify" "what is ("what are") the perceived barrier. Note that this is Descriptive *problem statement* and so it requires that descriptive *research design methodology* be used.

When we do research study on the physical growth and development of the child whether correlational or longitudinal, descriptive label will, for example, be used and the design will be multi-method. This will be justified by the fact that a lot descriptive information will be used before any other form of information is put into use. Descriptive research design is a scientific method which involves observing and describing the behavior of a subject without influencing it in any way.

Many scientific disciplines, especially social science and psychology, use this method to obtain a general overview of the subject. Some subjects cannot be observed in any other way; for example, a social case study of an individual subject is a descriptive research design and allows observation without affecting normal behavior. It is also useful where it is not possible to test and measure the large number of samples needed for more quantitative types of experimentation.

These types of experiments are often used by anthropologists, psychologists and social scientists to observe natural behaviors without affecting them in any way. It is also used by market researchers to judge the habits of customers, or by companies wishing to judge the morale of staff.

The results from a descriptive research can in no way be used as a definitive answer or to disprove a hypothesis but, if the limitations are understood, they can still be a useful tool in many areas of scientific research.

Let us look at some types of Survey research without dwelling into their detail but only touch the key aspect of the design. While these surveys are paper-and-pencil in nature (e.g., you're handed one or receive it in the mail and asked to fill it out and return it to the researcher), they are sometimes "administered" orally in a face-to-face or telephone interview (e.g., the researcher records your answers himself/herself).

There are other variations on survey-type questions; the above are just examples of the most common forms and scaling of such responses. If the responses to our earlier example were collected in the form of a survey -- be it, say, Likert-scaled attitudinal items and/or open-ended questions where the teachers are asked to share the perceived barriers in their own words -- then the study would be characterized as a *descriptive survey design methodology*.

Let us come back to *Observational* type where we said that in these research design methodologies, instead of administering a survey instrument, the researcher collects data by observing, tallying or recording the occurrence or incidence of some outcome (perhaps with the aid of assistants). The researcher might want to identify the most frequently occurring type(s) of disruptive behavior in a particular classroom. With clear prior agreement on what constitutes such "disruptive behavior", operational definitions of our variables are important). It becomes an issue of "reliability," or verifiability that *"I saw what I saw"* versus *"my own bias"* of what constitutes this disruptive behavior. The researcher could develop a listing of such behaviors and observe and record the number of times each one occurred in a particular observation session in a classroom. (Again, the researcher might wish to *'compare notes'* with those of assistants in order to enhance reliability or verifiability. That is as a *cross-check for accuracy.*

This type of research would warrant the design methodology label of not only "descriptive" due to the *'identify* or *what is – (what are)* but also "observational" due to the recording and /or tallying protocol. It is important to recognize that, qualitative-type observations can also be recorded. They don't have to be strictly numeric tallies. Examples of this nature include case notes of counselors, where they record their perceptions in words.

In Ex post facto(also called "causal comparative") we identify some sort of outcome and wonder 'what makes it vary like that. Could it be some pre-existing grouping? For instance, if we 'divided' or 'pile-sorted' the responses by gender, would that account for the difference we see?

48

Thus, there is no treatment either. Simply an attempt to see if a grouping that we had no prior control over seems to "make a difference" on some outcome(s). The keyword "difference" (by grouping) and no treatment would be the tip-off to an ex post facto or causal-comparative study design. And regarding the grouping, may be this rather silly example will make the point, and help you to identify if you are in such a situation of "no-control-over-grouping:" You wish to study whether preschoolers from single-parent homes are different in terms of emotional readiness for kindergarten than those of two-parent homes. Now you couldn't go to prospective subjects' homes and say, "OK, now you've got to get divorced or you have to stay married". You just leave the situation as "it is". Those subjects in essence are 'self-selected into their grouping. You had no prior control over 'making' them 'be' from this or that kind of a family background. Indeed the *literal Latin translation of "ex post facto" is "after the fact."* This shows your role in the 'grouping' process as the researcher. That is You didn't 'assign' them into any one group, randomly or otherwise. Instead, you came in "after the fact" and wished to see if that self-determined grouping made a difference on some outcome(s) that you are studying. Thus the name "causal comparative" is sort of a misnomer. You are indeed "comparing" two or more "pre-formed" groups on some outcome(s). But due to that lack of randomization and control, you can't really use this design to study "cause/effect" types of research questions or problem statements. There are generally too many *uncontrolled, unrandomized contaminating variables* that may have entered the picture to confidently make 'strong' cause/effect statements. Nonetheless, given the circumstances, this type of design might be "the best you can do." Group differences on some outcome(s) might indeed be interesting to study even though you had little or no "control" in the situation.

Correlation Research is a kind of research activities that attempts to identify correlation among variables. For example, we might wonder whether children's ages are correlated with their heights. To answer such questions, we might observe and record the heights of , say 100 children who vary in age from 2 years to 12 years and examine whether changes in the one variable correspond to changes in the other.. In this case, we may discover a clear correlation between the variables of age and height. That is, as children increase in age, they generally increase in height as well. This type of a relationship, in which the variables change in the same direction is describe d as *positive correlation* but where the variables move in opposite direction, we describe that as *negative correlation*. Finally, we may want to investigate the relationship between a child's height and the number of children in the child's classroom. In this case we would likely find that the two variable have no relationship at all and so we have *no correlation.* The strength of correlation can also be described- strong correlation implying that the variables in question are closely related. If the correlation is very weak, the predictability of one variable using the other becomes decreased. And when variables become completely unrelated, knowledge of one variable gives us NO clue of the other variable. The directions of relationship are given by plus (+) sign or minus (-) sign for positive and negative respectively. Where there is no correlation, we automatically assign Zero (0). The strength of relationship is called coefficient of correlation (r) whose strength ranges between +1.00 and -1.00. For example a correlation coefficient of + 0.87 indicates a strong positive correlation. We can also depict correlation graphically with *scatter diagram-* diagrams showing how the relationship between the variables are scattered. The scattering could be linear or otherwise. Correlation research, nevertheless, do play an important role in scientific research process. Like descriptive research, correlational studies are often sources of interesting and provocative questions which may be

49

formed into specific research hypotheses that investigators can go on to examine using more rigorous methods of research.

5.2 General Themes in Research

This section deals with the general themes of reliability and validity, standardization and the qualitative-quantitative dimension in research as discussed by H. Coolican, (1994), where he has briefly said the following:

- **Reliability** refers to a measure's consistency in producing similar results on different but comparable occasions.

- **Validity** ha to do with whether a measure is really measuring what it was intended to measure. In particular, for experimental work, there has bee a debate about *'threats to internal and external validity'*.

- **Internal Validity** refers to the issues of whether an effect was genuine or rather the result of incorrectly applied statistics, sampling biases or extraneous variables unconnected with the Internal Validity.

- **External Validity** concerns on whether an effect generalizes from specific people, place and measures of variables tested to the population, other populations, other places and to other, perhaps fuller, measures of the variables tested.

  It is in order for the student to study the various 'threats' and try to avoid them in practical work, or at least discuss them in writing about practical studies.

- **Standardized** procedures reduce Variance in people's performances, exclude bias from different treatment of groups and make **replication** possible. Replication is fundamental to the establishment of scientific credibility.

- The **qualitative –quantitative** dimension is introduced as a fundamental division within the theory of methods in contemporary psychological research. The dimension will be referred to throughout as research varies in the extent to which it employs aspects of either approach. Some researchers see the two approaches as complementary rather than antagonistic.

Whenever psychologists discuss measurement in the form of scales, tests, surveys, etc the issue arises of whether the measures are *reliable* and *valid*. Without going to deeper details, we need to discuss these two terms and get the general meaning of these terms.

5.3 Reliability

Reliability refers to a measure's consistency in producing similar results on different occasions. Any measure we use in file should be reliable, otherwise it's useless. You wouldn't want your car speedometer or a thermometer to give you different readings for the same values on different occasions. This applies to psychological measures as much as any other. Hence questionnaires should produce the same results when retested on the same people at different times and different observers measuring aggression in children should come up with similar ratings.

5.4 Validity

Validity has to do with whether a measure is really measuring what it was intended to measure. In addition to be consistent we should also be able to have confidence that our measuring device is measuring what it's supposed to measure. You wouldn't your speedometer to be recording oil pressure or your thermometer to be actually measuring humidity. In psychology, this issue is of absolutely crucial importance since, as you saw in the 'variables' chapter, it is often difficult to agree on what a concept 'really is' and things in psychology are not as touchable as things in physics or chemistry. Hence, validity is the issue of whether psychological measures really *do* make some assessment of the phenomenon under study.

5.5 Experimental Method

The general division of research design is that we have **Experimental** Design and **Non-Experimental** Research Design.

 > A **true experiment** occurs when an independent variable is manipulated and participants are randomly allocated to conditions.

 > **Quasi-experiments** occur when participants are not allocated by the experimenter into conditions of the manipulated independent variable.

 > Non-experiments investigate variables which exist among people irrespective of any researcher's intervention.

Among the variety of research methods and designs popular with psychological researchers, there is rather sharp divide. Designs are seen as either experimental or non-experimental, the latter often being called investigations too, in the general sense. This conceptual divide between methods is further sharpened by the fact that, in various learning institutions, it is possible to take a degree course in 'experimental psychology'.

Also a research **design** can be thought of as the structure of research. That is a design is what a researcher uses to structure the research, to show how all the major parts of the research will work together to try to address the research question, (Kombo& Tromp, 2006). It constitutes the blueprint for the collection, measurement and analysis of data Kothari,2003). A design is experimental if subjects are randomly assigned to treatment groups and to control (comparison) groups. Cook and Campbell (1979) mention ten types of experimental design. Note that the control group may receive no treatment, or it may be a group receiving a standard treatment (e.g., students receiving computer-supported instructions versus those receiving conventional instruction). That is, the control group is not necessarily one to be labeled "no treatment."

5.6 Nature of Experimental Method

In experiments, the ideal is to control all relevant variables whilst altering only the Independent Variable. A strong and careful attempt is made to even out random variables and to eliminate constant errors. The Reason given (H.Coolican, 1994) for this is that, if all other variables are controlled; only the Independent Variable can be responsible for change in the Dependent Variable. This reasoning is not restricted to scientific experiment but is used as "common-sense' thinking in many practical situations in daily life. For example, if you are trying to work out what is causing the interference on the starting on your car, you would probably try checking the battery, leaving all other parts of the car as they were, and if the battery is okay, you check the fuse related to ignition, and so on until the interference stops.

Many criticisms exist on Experimental method, involving the implicit assumption that the experiment is being carried out in a laboratory. Even those who strongly favor the use of experimental method have realized that there are very many pitfalls involved in running experiments, some of which are not obvious and have been brought to our attention by sometimes dramatic demonstrations. The following are some of the criticisms that apply to the experiment as a design, irrespective of where it is carried out, as documented by Barber,(197).

- Investigator paradigm effect

- Investigator experimental design effect

- Investigator loose procedure effect

- Investigator data analysis effect

- Investigator fudging effect

- Experimenter personal attributes effect

- Experimenter failure to follow the procedure effect

- Experimenter misrecording effect

- Experimenter fudging effect

- Experimenter unintentional expectancy effect

Most of these do not need clarification since they speak for themselves and several could be applied to non-experimental studies.

5.7 Design of Experimental Method

Basic experimental designs can be used in psychological research along with their various strengths and weaknesses.
Let us discuss the main points so that we understand these strengths and weaknesses using the table given here below.

5.8 Observational Methods

In a sense, all data from people are gathered through some form of observation but for instance, data gathered through questionnaire or interview deserves separate treatment.

A set of methods which can avoid some, but not always all, of these critisms is the set known generally as 'observational methods'. Behaviour is observed in every psychological study. A researcher makes observations on the participants' reaction times, answers to a questionnaire, memory performance and so on. There is ambiguity in using the term 'observational' in research literature. It can refer to the use of observation as a technique for gathering data about behavior within an experimental design. On the other hand, 'observational' might describe the overall design of a study, in contrast to a controlled experiment. We can look at observation as a Technique and as an overall Design.

5.9 Comparison Studies

Generally, Comparison studies will imply 'Comparison Groups' which is not different from talking about 'Control groups'. Most quasi-experiments protect against one threat to internal validity while risking another. A true experiment controls for both time-related and group-related threats. The two features that mark true experiments are two or more differently treated groups and randomly assignment to these groups. These features require that the researchers have control over the experimental treatment and the power to place subjects in groups. Thus, True Experiments employ both treated and control groups to deal with time-related rival explanations. A Control group reflects changes occurring during the time of study other than those due to treatment.Briefly talking about "experiments" generally, in terms of "key features" such as:

a) **Tight control** where the researcher attempts to identify in advance as many possible 'contaminating' and/or confounding variables as possible and to control for them in his/her design by building them in and balancing on them, for example, equal numbers of boys and girls to 'control for gender and/ or 'randomizing them away' by drawing a random sample of subjects and thereby 'getting a good mix' on them, e.g., all levels of 'socioeconomic status' we can say the researcher is on comparison studies.
b) because of the preceding control, the 'confidence' to **make 'cause/effect statements'**

That is, we begin to get the idea of *two or more groups, as balanced and equivalent as possible on all but one "thing:" our "treatment"* e.g., type of lesson, type of counseling need to be *measured before and after this treatment and if we do find a difference in the group that 'got the treatment,' we hope to attribute that difference to the treatment only* (because of this tight control, randomization, and so forth).

There are actually two "sub-types" of experimental designs. Plainly put, they have to do with how much 'control' or 'power' you as the researcher have to do the above randomization and grouping!

5.10 True experimental

If you can both randomly draw (select) individuals for your study and then randomly assign these individuals to two or more groups (e.g., 'you have the power to make the groups' yourself!), then you have what is known as a true experiment.'

53

The procedure is from the entire population, the researcher randomly selects the subjects and randomly assigns the subjects to experiments and leaves other groups as control groups. **See Fig.A1 below as presented in Wikipedia (2010)**

Fig.A1

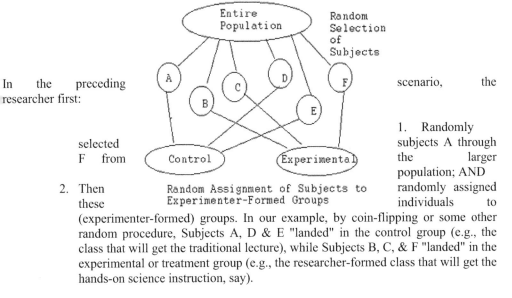

In the preceding researcher first: scenario, the

1. Randomly selected subjects A through F from the larger population; AND randomly assigned individuals to

2. Then these (experimenter-formed) groups. In our example, by coin-flipping or some other random procedure, Subjects A, D & E "landed" in the control group (e.g., the class that will get the traditional lecture), while Subjects B, C, & F "landed" in the experimental or treatment group (e.g., the researcher-formed class that will get the hands-on science instruction, say).

The two levels of "randomization" help to ensure good control of those pesky contaminating or confounding variables. You're more likely to get a "good mix" on all those other factors when you can randomly draw your subjects and also randomly assign them to groups that you as the researcher have the "power" to form. What if you get the OK to do your research within a school district, but the District Education Officer In-Charge comes and says "Oh no I can't let you be disrupting our bureaucratic organization here and "making your own 4th grade classrooms for your study. That is too disruptive."

The best you can do to counteract the threat is to randomly select INTACT existing

4th grade classrooms and then go ahead and use all the kids in those randomly drawn

GROUPS instead.

5.11 The True Experiment and Quasi-Experiment

Which brings us to the 2nd variant of "experimental designs:"

B. Quasi-experimental - what you are 'randomly drawing' (selecting) is Not Individuals but Intact (pre-existing) Groups. These could be existing classrooms, clinics, vocational education centers, etc. In other words, you "lose" the power to "make your own groups" for your study. Study Fig A2 below

Fig A2

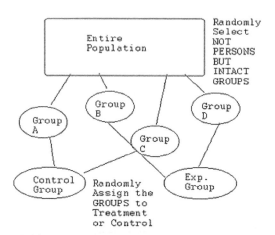

Here (for the quasi-experiment), you randomly draw intact groups (e.g., from all the 4th grades in the district, you draw 4 of them at random) and then flip a coin or use some other random procedure to assign the pre-existing 4th grades to either the "treatment" or "control" conditions. (In our example Grades A and C "land" in the traditional lecture method (control), while Grades B and D end up in the hands-on science instruction (e.g., the "treatment" or the "experimental" group).

Do you see how this is different from the "true" experiment? In the "true" experiment, you selected the children themselves (subjects) at random and then "had the power" to in essence "form" your own "4th grades" by assigning the individual kids themselves randomly to either the control or the experimental conditions.

Here, though, the 'best you can do' (again, often for practical reasons such as access to sites, permission, etc.) is draw not individual kids but the groups themselves (pre-existing 4th grade classrooms) at random and then in step 2 assigning NOT the individual kids but rather the whole groups to either the treatment or control conditions.

Open the link below for more detailed information about Quasi-Experimental design

5.12 Quasi-Experimental Design

This one-step loss of randomization may mean a bit less control over those contaminants. By forming your own groups you have a greater likelihood of "getting a good mix on all other stuff".

But here, you've got to "live with the existing groups as is." And suppose that in the above scenario, 4th Grades B & D also happen (quite by accident, but welcome to 'real life') to have a higher average I.Q. of 15 points than A & B. Now we've got a contaminant. Did the kids do better because of the hands-on science lesson -- or because of their inherently higher aptitude, intelligence or whatever? But at least we still have that last step: random assignment to either the experimental or control conditions. Remember:-

1. For true experiments, we're randomly assigning individuals to treatment vs. control; and
2. For quasi-experiments, we're randomly assigning intact/pre-existing groups to treatment vs. control.

We lose that "random assignment" property in the 3rd "family" of group comparison design methodologies!

Ex post facto (also called "causal comparative")- really no 'random anything!' We identify some sort of outcome and wonder 'what makes it vary like that?' Could it be some pre-existing grouping? For instance, if we 'divided' or 'pile-sorted' the responses by gender, would that account for the difference we see? Thus, there is no treatment either! Simply an attempt to see if a grouping that we had no prior control over seems to "make a difference" on some outcome(s)! The keyword "difference" (by grouping) and no treatment would be the tip-off to an ex post facto or causal-comparative study design.

And -- regarding the grouping -- maybe this rather silly example will make the point! And help you to identify if you are in such a situation of "no-control-over-grouping:"

You wish to study whether preschoolers from single-parent homes are different in terms of emotional readiness for kindergarten than those of two-parent homes.

Now, you couldn't go to prospective subjects' homes and say, "OK, now you've got to get divorced; and YOU have to stay married because that is how you can come up in the random assignment."

I don't think so. Same thing with "gender:" you took it "as is" (e.g., those subjects in essence 'self-selected into their gender grouping). You had no prior control over 'making' them 'be' one gender or the other but rather took those groups 'as is' and kind of pile-sorted some response(s) by gender to see if it 'made a difference' on some outcome! Indeed ... the *literal Latin translation of "ex post facto" is "after the fact."* This shows Your role in the 'grouping' process as the researcher. You didn't 'assign' them into any one group, randomly or otherwise. Instead, you came in "after the fact" and wished to see if that self-determined grouping made a difference on some outcome(s) that you are studying. As you can imagine even bigger problems with contaminating variables. There is no randomization or control here.

Thus the name "causal comparative" is sort of a misnomer. You are indeed "comparing" two or more "pre-formed" groups on some outcome(s). But due to that *lack of randomization and control*, you can't really use this design to study "cause-effect" types of research questions or problem statements. There are generally *too many uncontrolled, unrandomized contaminating variables* that may have entered the picture to confidently make 'strong' cause-effect statements.

Nonetheless, given the circumstances, this type of design might be "the best you can do." Group differences on some outcome(s) might indeed be interesting to study even though you had little or no "control" in the situation.

5.13 Cross-Sectional Studies

Both these and longitudinal studies can give information on changes in a psychological variable over time. A cross-sectional study does this by taking groups of children or adults from different specified age bands and comparing them at the same moment in time. Comparisons may well highlight age-related changes and developmental trends. Cross-sectional data are often used to support developmental theories such as those of Piaget or Freud.Cross-sectional study can also compare groups defined other than by age. A cross-section of a classes might be studied, or of occupational or ethnic groups but always comparing the samples at the same time.

5.14 Longitudinal Studies

The big disadvantage of cross sectional studies is that is of comparability, a problem encountered in any study using independent samples. We can't ever be sure that our two or more groups are similar enough for fair comparison. The longitudinal approach surmounts this difficulty since it employs repeated measures on the same group of people over a substantial period, often a number of years. In this way genuine changes and the stability of some characteristics may be observed. If intervals between observations are not too large, major points of change can be identified.

References

1. Blaxter, L. Hughes, C. & Tight, M. (1998) How to Research.Buckingham: Open University Press.

2. Creswell, John W. (2002). *Research design: Qualitative, quantitative, and mixed methods approach,* **Publisher:** SAGE Publications, Inc;

3. Collis, J. & Hussey, R. (2003) *Business Research: a practical guidefor   undergraduate and postgraduate students, second edition.*Basingstoke: Palgrave Macmillan.

4. Denscombe, M. (2002) *Ground Rules for Good Research,*Maidenhead: Open University Press.

5. Duncan and Duncan (1994).*Multivariate Behavioral Research, Modeling incomplete longitudinal substance use using latent growth curve methodology.* Behavioral Research,29:4,313-338,DOI: 10.1207/s15327906mbr2904_1

6. Gill, J. & Johnson, P. (1997) *Research Methods for Manager* (2nd edition), London: Paul Chapman.
7. Henry, G.T. (1990) *Practical Sampling*, Newbury Park, CA, Sage.

8. Kerlinger F.N. (2004). *Foundations of Behavioral Research*, Surjeet Publications, India

9. Kombo, D., K and D .L.A. Tromp (2006*), Proposal and Thesis Writing An Introduction.Paulines Publications, Africa Kenya*

10. Kervin, J.B. (1992) *Methods for Business Research.* NY: HarperCollins
11. Rosenthal, R. (1966) *Experimenter Effects in Behavioural Research.*N.Y. Appleton-Century-Crofts.
12. Saunders, M, Lewis, P. &Thornhill, A. (2007) *Research Methods forBusiness Students* (4th edition) Harlow: Prentice Hall.
13. Silverman, D. (1993) *Interpreting Qualitative Data: Methods forAnalysing Talk, Text and Interaction.* London: Sage.
14. *Torrington, D. (1991)* management Face to Face. *London: PrenticeHall*

15. Thomas D. and Donald T. Campbell. (1979).*Quasi-experimentation: Design and analysis issues for field settings,* Cook,

16. Vasta, Haith and Miller, (1992). *Child Psychology- The Modern Science.NY: John Wiley &Sons, Inc*

Printed in Great Britain
by Amazon

81202969R00038